LOOKING FORWARD

Filter Bubbles and Targeted Advertising

THE NEW YORK TIMES EDITORIAL STAFF

Published in 2020 by New York Times Educational Publishing
in association with The Rosen Publishing Group, Inc.
29 East 21st Street, New York, NY 10010

First Edition

The New York Times
Alex Ward: Editorial Director, Book Development
Phyllis Collazo: Photo Rights/Permissions Editor
Heidi Giovine: Administrative Manager

Rosen Publishing
Megan Kellerman: Managing Editor
Michael Hessel-Mial: Editor
Greg Tucker: Creative Director
Brian Garvey: Art Director

Cataloging-in-Publication Data
Names: New York Times Company.
Title: Filter bubbles and targeted advertising / edited by the New
York Times editorial staff.
Description: New York : New York Times Educational Publishing,
2020. | Series: Looking forward | Includes glossary and index.
Identifiers: ISBN 9781642822694 (library bound) | ISBN
9781642822687 (pbk.) | ISBN 9781642822700 (ebook)
Subjects: LCSH: Filter bubbles (Information filtering)—Juvenile
literature. | Advertising—Juvenile literature. | Media literacy—
Juvenile literature.
Classification: LCC ZA3085.F558 2020 | DDC 025.5'24—dc23

Manufactured in the United States of America

On the cover: Filter bubbles, which exclude other perspectives
from our tech-assisted preferences, reveal the future challenges
of a personalized, automated web; Logorilla/istockphoto.

Contents

Political Uses of the Personalized Web

Tech Companies Under Scrutiny

Introduction

THE HISTORY OF the Internet is the history of solutions to engineering challenges: linking computers, searching for information, connecting with users or presenting content in novel ways. The companies with successful solutions have been rewarded not just with profits but with enormous influence over how people use them. One such solution is the personalized web, in which platforms filter and recommend content fitted to our preferences. This new web has changed society, positively and negatively, well beyond our computer screens. The coming years will determine how everyday users respond to these changes.

The story begins with Google, which over a decade ago had already transformed the Internet with the convenience of its search engine. Though not yet personalized, Google's search function would shape commerce, media and politics to fit its architecture. People began crafting their websites to improve their ranking in Google's system. A pattern was set: A platform finds success by offering desired content to users, and in the process the web changes to fit the platform.

At the same time, companies such as Netflix and Amazon began introducing recommendations to their platforms. Facebook and Google followed suit with a personalized news feed and search. How do these companies achieve this personalization? The answer lies in algorithms that predict our choices based on the statistical analysis of large data sets. These algorithms rely on "collaborative filtering," which uses peer choices as a basis for recommendation. Building data profiles on every user, algorithms determine the likelihood of a purchase or click based on the categories our profiles fit into. Platforms then generate additional revenue by selling this data to advertisers.

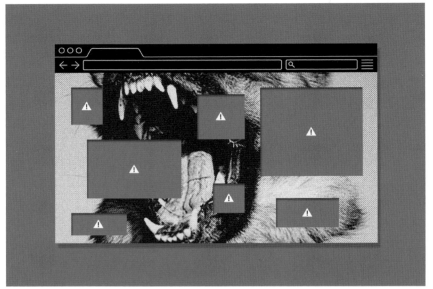

As a result, the Internet is dominated by a small number of platforms that deliver content tailored to each consumer. One beneficiary, other than the platforms themselves, was e-commerce; specialized services could find their niche and sell to it. But over this rapid process, the resulting data footprint grew. The average user had little ability to track what had been collected on them and to whom that data was sold. While the European Union maintained strict digital privacy laws, the United States made few demands on behalf of digital consumers.

Journalism changed, too, especially due to Facebook, whose ever-changing algorithms could make or break media outlets by redirecting the traffic of millions of users. Chasing digital advertising revenue, traditional outlets and newcomers alike were forced to change their style. Lower-tier publications began writing "clickbait" headlines to maximize site visits — even if the article didn't fulfill expectations. Other outlets laid off writers to prioritize video or blended content and advertising in a new form of product placement called "native advertising." Though strong journalism continued, objective reporting and the working conditions of journalists suffered.

The changes brought about by the personalized Internet have a pattern, which activist Eli Pariser named "the filter bubble." Filter bubbles are the effect of only seeing content that fits one's worldview, whether it is the same few genres of music or news articles that fit one perspective. Pariser's point, which the articles in this collection support, is that the filter bubble is not simply a result of personal taste but of digital platforms inadvertently limiting users' media diets.

During the 2016 elections, the Internet became a battleground on which the filter bubble became a weapon. Many observers noticed the rise of "fake news," inflammatory and poorly sourced partisan news that circulated broadly. Much of it was created by content farms for advertising revenue, selling left or right wing news to the echo chambers that craved it. Likewise, The New York Times reported that Cambridge Analytica, in collaboration with the Trump campaign, used personal data from millions of people without their consent. This allowed the campaign to target ads to undecided voters.

During the election and afterward, people started asking questions. How were these platforms affecting media and public discourse? What responsibility do they have to the public? What rights do citizens have over how their data is used? And lastly, is this the only way for the Internet to be? Conservative commentator Ross Douthat observed that Facebook and other platforms had turned the Internet into a "subtle empire." He argued that, regardless of one's political views, one must consider the effects these platforms have on our society.

As the Internet evolves, we will continue to see new tools that add unexpected value to our lives. At the same time, those tools will shape our behavior and worldview, as changes in media always have. Reflecting on the personalized web and the aftermath of what it brought about, it is worth remembering that as the Internet can change us, so can we, in turn, remake the web.

CHAPTER 1

Digital Platforms Personalize Our Online Experience

In the first decade of the 21st century, Google became the most popular search engine. Its proprietary search algorithm ranked pages by relevant keywords and by the number of times a site was linked by other pages. This method, and the resulting control over web traffic, started to shape e-commerce, news media and politics in Google's image. By the end of the decade, algorithms like Google's (as well as those of services like Amazon and Netflix) began to successfully generate personalized recommendations for their products, opening the door to the personalized web.

This Boring Headline Is Written for Google

BY STEVE LOHR | APRIL 9, 2006

JOURNALISTS OVER THE YEARS have assumed they were writing their headlines and articles for two audiences — fickle readers and nitpicking editors. Today, there is a third important arbiter of their work: the software programs that scour the Web, analyzing and ranking online news articles on behalf of Internet search engines like Google, Yahoo and MSN.

The search-engine "bots" that crawl the Web are increasingly influential, delivering 30 percent or more of the traffic on some newspaper, magazine or television news Web sites. And traffic means readers and advertisers, at a time when the mainstream media is desperately trying to make a living on the Web.

So news organizations large and small have begun experimenting with tweaking their Web sites for better search engine results. But software bots are not your ordinary readers: They are blazingly fast yet numbingly literal-minded. There are no algorithms for wit, irony, humor or stylish writing. The software is a logical, sequential, left-brain reader, while humans are often right brain.

In newspapers and magazines, for example, section titles and headlines are distilled nuggets of human brainwork, tapping context and culture. "Part of the craft of journalism for more than a century has been to think up clever titles and headlines, and Google comes along and says, 'The heck with that,' " observed Ed Canale, vice president for strategy and new media at The Sacramento Bee.

Moves to accommodate the technology are tricky. How far can a news organization go without undercutting its editorial judgment concerning the presentation, tone and content of news?

So far, the news media are gingerly stepping into the field of "search engine optimization." It is a booming business, estimated at $1.25 billion in revenue worldwide last year, and projected to more than double this year.

Much of this revenue comes from e-commerce businesses, whose sole purpose is to sell goods and services online. For these sites, search engine optimization has become a constant battle of one-upmanship, pitting the search engine technologists against the marketing experts and computer scientists working for the Web sites.

Think of it as an endless chess game. The optimizer wizards devise some technical trick to outwit the search-engine algorithms that rank the results of a search. The search engines periodically change their algorithms to thwart such self-interested manipulation, and the game starts again.

News organizations, by contrast, have moved cautiously. Mostly, they are making titles and headlines easier for search engines to find and fathom. About a year ago, The Sacramento Bee changed online section titles. "Real Estate" became "Homes," "Scene" turned into "Lifestyle," and dining information found in newsprint under "Taste" is online under "Taste/Food."

Some news sites offer two headlines. One headline, often on the first Web page, is clever, meant to attract human readers. Then, one click to a second Web page, a more quotidian, factual headline appears with the article itself. The popular BBC News Web site does this routinely on longer articles.

Nic Newman, head of product development and technology at BBC News Interactive, pointed to a few examples from last Wednesday. The first headline a human reader sees: "Unsafe sex: Has Jacob Zuma's rape trial hit South Africa's war on AIDS?" One click down: "Zuma testimony sparks HIV fear." Another headline meant to lure the human reader: "Tulsa star: The life and career of much-loved 1960's singer." One click down: "Obituary: Gene Pitney."

"The search engine has to get a straightforward, factual headline, so it can understand it," Mr. Newman said. With a little programming sleight-of-hand, the search engine can be steered first to the straightforward, somewhat duller headline, according to some search optimizers.

On the Web, space limitations can coincide with search-engine preferences. In the print version of The New York Times, an article last Tuesday on Florida beating U.C.L.A. for the men's college basketball championship carried a longish headline, with allusions to sports history: "It's Chemistry Over Pedigree as Gators Roll to First Title." On the Times Web site, whose staff has undergone some search-engine optimization training, the headline of the article was, "Gators Cap Run With First Title."

The Associated Press, which feeds articles to 11,000 newspapers, radio and television stations, limits its online headlines to less than 40 characters, a concession to small screens. And on the Web, there is added emphasis on speed and constant updates.

"You put those demands, and that you know you're also writing for search engines, and you tend to write headlines that are more straightforward," said Lou Ferrara, online editor of The Associated Press. "My worry is that some creativity is lost."

Whether search engines will influence journalism below the headline is uncertain. The natural-language processing algorithms, search experts say, scan the title, headline and at least the first hundred words or so of news articles.

Journalists, they say, would be wise to do a little keyword research to determine the two or three most-searched words that relate to their subject — and then include them in the first few sentences. "That's not something they teach in journalism schools," said Danny Sullivan, editor of SearchEngineWatch, an online newsletter. "But in the future, they should."

Such suggestions stir mixed sentiments. "My first thought is that reporters and editors have a job to do and they shouldn't worry about what Google's or Yahoo's software thinks of their work," said Michael Schudson, a professor at the University of California, San Diego, who is a visiting faculty member at the Columbia University Graduate School of Journalism.

"But my second thought is that newspaper headlines and the presentation of stories in print are in a sense marketing devices to bring readers to your story," Mr. Schudson added. "Why not use a new marketing device appropriate to the age of the Internet and the search engine?"

In journalism, as in other fields, the tradition of today was once an innovation. The so-called inverted pyramid structure of a news article — placing the most important information at the top — was shaped in part by a new technology of the 19th century, the telegraph, the Internet of its day. Putting words on telegraph wires was costly, so reporters made sure the most significant points were made at the start.

Yet it wasn't all technological determinism by any means. The inverted pyramid style of journalism, according to Mr. Schudson, became standard practice only in 1900, four decades or more after telegraph networks came into use. It awaited the rise of journalists as "an avowedly independent, self-conscious, professionalizing group," confident of their judgments about what information was most important, he said.

The new technology shaped practice, but people determined how the technology was used — and it took a while. Something similar is the likely path of the Internet.

"We're all struggling and experimenting with how news is presented in the future," said Larry Kramer, president of CBS Digital Media. "And there's nothing wrong with search engine optimization as long as it doesn't interfere with news judgment. It shouldn't, and it's up to us to make sure it doesn't. But it is a tool that is part of being effective in this medium."

A New Campaign Tactic: Manipulating Google Data

BY TOM ZELLER JR. | OCT. 26, 2006

IF THINGS GO AS PLANNED for liberal bloggers in the next few weeks, searching Google for "Jon Kyl," the Republican senator from Arizona now running for re-election, will produce high among the returns a link to an April 13 article from The Phoenix New Times, an alternative weekly.

Mr. Kyl "has spent his time in Washington kowtowing to the Bush administration and the radical right," the article suggests, "very often to the detriment of Arizonans."

Searching Google for "Peter King," the Republican congressman from Long Island, would bring up a link to a Newsday article headlined "King Endorses Ethnic Profiling."

Fifty or so other Republican candidates have also been made targets in a sophisticated "Google bombing" campaign intended to game the search engine's ranking algorithms. By flooding the Web with references to the candidates and repeatedly cross-linking to specific articles and sites on the Web, it is possible to take advantage of Google's formula and force those articles to the top of the list of search results.

The project was originally aimed at 70 Republican candidates but was scaled back to roughly 50 because Chris Bowers, who conceived it, thought some of the negative articles too partisan.

The articles to be used "had to come from news sources that would be widely trusted in the given district," said Mr. Bowers, a contributor at MyDD.com (Direct Democracy), a liberal group blog. "We wanted actual news reports so it would be clear that we weren't making anything up."

Each name is associated with one article. Those articles are embedded in hyperlinks that are now being distributed widely among the left-leaning blogosphere. In an entry at MyDD.com this week,

Mr. Bowers said: "When you discuss any of these races in the future, please, use the same embedded hyperlink when reprinting the Republican's name. Then, I suppose, we will see what happens."

An accompanying part of the project is intended to buy up Google Adwords, so that searches for the candidates' names will bring up advertisements that point to the articles as well. But Mr. Bowers said his hopes for this were fading, because he was very busy.

The ability to manipulate the search engine's results has been demonstrated in the past. Searching for "miserable failure," for example, produces the official Web site of President Bush.

But it is far from clear whether this particular campaign will be successful. Much depends on the extent of political discussion already tied to a particular candidate's name.

It will be harder to manipulate results for searches of the name of a candidate who has already been widely covered in the news and widely discussed in the blogosphere, because so many links and so many pages already refer to that particular name. Search results on lesser-known candidates, with a smaller body of references and links, may be easier to change.

"We don't condone the practice of Google bombing, or any other action that seeks to affect the integrity of our search results," said Ricardo Reyes, a Google spokesman. "A site's ranking in Google's search results is automatically determined by computer algorithms using thousands of factors to calculate a page's relevance to a given query."

The company's faith in its system has produced a hands-off policy when it comes to correcting for the effects of Google bombs in the past. Over all, Google says, the integrity of the search product remains intact.

Writing in the company's blog last year, Marissa Mayer, Google's director of consumer Web products, suggested that pranks might be "distracting to some, but they don't affect the overall quality of our search service, whose objectivity, as always, remains the core of our mission."

Still, some conservative blogs have condemned Mr. Bowers's tactic. These include Outside the Beltway, which has called him "unscrupulous," and Hot Air, which declared the effort "fascinatingly evil."

But Mr. Bowers suggested that he was acting with complete transparency and said he hoped political campaigns would take up the tactic, which he called "search engine optimization," as a standard part of their arsenal.

"I did this out in the open using my real name, using my own Web site," he said. "There's no hidden agenda. One of the reasons for this is to show that campaigns should be doing this on their own."

Indeed, if all campaigns were doing it, the playing field might well be leveled.

Mr. Bowers said he did not believe the practice would actually deceive most Internet users.

"I think Internet users are very smart and most are aware of what a Google bomb is," he said, "and they will be aware that results can be massaged a bit."

Researchers Track Down a Plague of Fake Web Pages

BY JOHN MARKOFF | MARCH 19, 2007

TENS OF THOUSANDS of junk Web pages, created only to lure search-engine users to advertisements, are proliferating like billboards strung along freeways. Now Microsoft researchers say they have traced the companies and techniques behind them.

A technical paper published by the researchers says the links promoting such pages are generated by a small group of shadowy operators apparently with the acquiescence of some major advertisers, Web page hosts and advertising syndicators. The report is available at www.cs.ucdavis.edu/~hchen/paper/www07.pdf.

The finding is striking because it hints at the possibility of curbing the practice.

The researchers uncovered a complex scheme in which a small group, creating false doorway pages, works with operators of Web-based computers who profit by redirecting traffic passed from search engines in one direction and then sending advertisements acquired from syndicators in the opposite direction.

"A small number of rogue actors who know what they are doing can create an enormous amount of disruption," said David L. Sifry, chief executive of Technorati, a blog-indexing company that works to keep junk pages of this sort out of its indexes. "It's sort of like putting a blindfold on you and spinning you around three times and then taking off the blindfold and showing you an ad."

Using questionable or illegal techniques to improve the ranking of a Web site in query results is known as search-engine spamming. The practice has proved to be a vexing problem for the major search companies, which struggle to prevent both spammers and companies specializing in improving legitimate clients' Web traffic — a field known as search-engine optimization — from undermining their page-ranking systems.

Surprisingly, the researchers noted that the vast bulk of the junk listings was created from just two Web hosting companies and that as many as 68 percent of the advertisements sampled were placed by just three advertising syndicators.

Search-engine spam is a small but growing component of the overall spam problem, which is predominantly junk e-mail sent from millions of Internet-connected home PCs that have been infected with malicious software. The overall amount of e-mail spam has more than doubled in the last year, according to Postini, a communications security firm.

Mr. Sifry said search-engine spam might be more controllable because of the improved accountability of the Web. "I am actually optimistic about squashing all of this, or at least making sure that it is manageable," he said.

The Microsoft paper was distributed by Yi-Min Wang and Ming Ma, cybersecurity investigators in the company's research division, in

STUART ISETT FOR THE NEW YORK TIMES

Yi-Min Wang of Microsoft helped track the source of the Web pages.

collaboration with Yuan Niu and Hao Chen, computer scientists at the University of California, Davis.

The researchers found that for some keywords like "drugs" and "ring tone," more than 30 percent of the results from major search engines were fake pages created by spammers.

They discovered that the average spam density — a measure of the percentage of Web pages that contain only advertisements — was 11 percent for 1,000 keywords they used in their research.

The researchers said large advertisers were to blame for a significant share of the spam problem.

"Ultimately, it is advertisers' money that is funding the search-spam industry, which is increasingly cluttering the Web with low-quality content and reducing Web users' productivity," they write in the paper, which will be presented in May at the International World Wide Web Conference in Banff, Alberta.

Mr. Wang, group manager and senior researcher for cybersecurity and systems management at Microsoft, said, "The good guys are part of the problem."

The researchers' specific findings included evidence that some blog-hosting services have permitted an explosion of phony doorway pages. For example, the researchers noted that such pages were far more prevalent in Google's blogspot.com service than in other hosting domains. The Microsoft Research team has worked extensively with the managers of Microsoft's Spaces blog-hosting service to detect and identify search-engine spam, Mr. Wang said. Google would not comment for the record on its own efforts to combat such practices.

The Microsoft research findings, based on a survey in October, also determined that much of the spam ad traffic was being funneled through the Internet addresses of just two Web-hosting companies.

Phillip Rosenthal, chief technology officer of one of the companies, ISPrime, an Internet services company based in New York, said the activity had been traced to a single customer and violated the company's acceptable-use policy. He said the company's relationship with the customer, whom he would not identify, had been severed after the company was notified about the Microsoft paper by a reporter.

But he was also pessimistic about permanently stopping operators who subvert search engines to gain advertising revenue in this way.

Guessing the Online Customer's Next Want

BY ERIC A. TAUB | MAY 19, 2008

MARKETERS HAVE ALWAYS tried to predict what people want, and then get them to buy it.

Among online retailers, pushing customers toward other products they might want is a common practice. Both Amazon and Netflix, two of the best-known practitioners of targeted upselling, have long recommended products or movie titles to their clientele. They do so using a technique called collaborative filtering, basing suggestions on customers' previous purchases and on how they rate products compared to other consumers.

Figuring that out is not so easy. For one thing, people do not always buy what they like. Someone may buy a sweater for their grandmother even though they dislike it and would never get it again. Similarly, a person who rents a movie may actually detest it but knows her child likes it. Or a film that was seen on a small airplane screen may garner a lower rating than if it were seen at a large multiplex.

The search for a better recommendation continues with numerous companies selling algorithms that promise a retailer more of an edge. For instance, Barneys New York, the upscale clothing store chain, says it got at least a 10 percent increase in online revenue by using data mining software that finds links between certain online behavior and a greater propensity to buy.

Using a system developed by Proclivity Systems, Barneys used data about where and when a customer visited its site and other demographic information to determine on whom it should focus its e-mail messages.

For instance, an e-mail message announcing sales might go to those Web site visitors who had purchased certain products or types of products in the past, but who had done so only when the items were on sale. In the simplest terms, if someone buys only when something is on sale, but never buys anything in December, then the e-mail sale flier might not be sent to that customer in December. "There is a digital trail of interest left by customers," said Sheldon Gilbert, Proclivity's chief executive and founder.

The observation about sales could be integrated with other behavior. Does the customer buy only when an item reaches a certain price? Is the customer more likely to buy on a weekend or during the week? Must it be organic material? An algorithm would weigh those behaviors to determine the likelihood that someone will open the e-mail message, and once opened, decide to click through to the site and buy the product. The more data, the better it gets at predicting, says Proclivity, which is based in New York.

"One customer found that 10 percent of its population accounted for 60 percent of bargain sales. So on the day of the sale, you can send a full-price ad to everyone else," said Mr. Gilbert.

Barneys experienced at least a 10 percent increase in online revenue, as compared to control groups, said Larry Promisel, Barneys' vice president of e-commerce. It found 20 percent more customers would purchase once sent the targeted e-mail messages. The company has saved money by not sending e-mail letters to customers unlikely to buy.

Not only are sales increasing, Mr. Promisel said, but with the store focusing on customers with items they are likely to buy, its clientele feels that it understands their interests, which increases good will.

Still, the problem of knowing what people want is hardly solved. While Netflix has persuaded almost five million subscribers to provide two billion movie ratings to its site, the company still has trouble figuring out exactly what somebody will like.

"I wish I could tell you that our recommendations system was reliable, but it's not perfect," said Reed Hastings, Netflix's chief executive.

At best, Netflix knows that if someone rates a particular drama highly, it can predict what other drama they might like by correlating one's rating of that film with others. "But if I know your taste in drama, I do not know your taste in horror," Mr. Hastings said.

As customers value selection and rapid delivery more than recommendations, the company is not that worried about its prediction system. Even a 10 percent improvement of its ratings system has not been possible. Netflix has offered a $1 million prize to anyone who can do that, but to date, only slightly better than a 9 percent improvement has been achieved.

"Using as much information as you can is very important," said Yehuda Koren, an AT&T Labs researcher, who was part of the group that achieved the results. To do even better, Mr. Koren would "track all clicks, the movies that people searched for, the pages they jumped to, their mouse movements," information that Netflix does not now collect.

Doing this type of analysis, Mr. Gilbert of Proclivity believes, would stop retailers from sending out buying recommendations based on outdated information.

"I still get e-mails from Amazon recommending books based on the Jared Diamond titles I bought three years ago," he said. "But I get nothing about my interest in gardening."

If You Liked This, You're Sure to Love That

BY CLIVE THOMPSON | NOV. 21, 2008

THE "NAPOLEON DYNAMITE" problem is driving Len Bertoni crazy. Bertoni is a 51-year-old "semiretired" computer scientist who lives an hour outside Pittsburgh. In the spring of 2007, his sister-in-law e-mailed him an intriguing bit of news: Netflix, the Web-based DVD-rental company, was holding a contest to try to improve Cinematch, its "recommendation engine." The prize: $1 million.

Cinematch is the bit of software embedded in the Netflix Web site that analyzes each customer's movie-viewing habits and recommends other movies that the customer might enjoy. (Did you like the legal thriller "The Firm"? Well, maybe you'd like "Michael Clayton." Or perhaps "A Few Good Men.") The Netflix Prize goes to anyone who can make Cinematch's predictions 10 percent more accurate. One million dollars might sound like an awfully big prize for such a small improvement. But in fact, Netflix's founders tried for years to improve Cinematch, with only incremental results, and they knew that a 10 percent bump would be a challenge for even the most deft programmer. They also knew that, as Reed Hastings, the chief executive of Netflix, told me recently, "getting to 10 percent would certainly be worth well in excess of $1 million" to the company. The competition was announced in October 2006, and no one has won yet, though 30,000 hackers worldwide are hard at work on the problem. Each day, teams submit their updated solutions to the Netflix Prize Web page, and Netflix instantly calculates how much better than Cinematch they are. (There's even a live "leader board" ranking the top contestants.)

In March 2007, Bertoni decided he wanted to give it a crack. So he downloaded a huge set of data that Netflix put online: an enormous list showing how 480,189 of the company's customers rated 17,770 Netflix movies. When Netflix customers log into their accounts, they can rate any movie from one to five stars, to help "teach" the Netflix system what their preferences are; the average customer has rated around 200 movies, so Netflix has a lot of information about what its customers like and don't like. (The data set doesn't include any personal information — names, ages, location and gender have been stripped out.) So Bertoni began looking for patterns that would predict customer behavior — specifically, an algorithm that would guess correctly the number of stars a given user would apply to a given movie. A year and a half later, Bertoni is still going, often spending 20 hours a week working on it in his home office. His two children — 12 and 13 years old — sometimes sit and brainstorm with him. "They're very good with mathematics and algebra," he told me, chuckling. "And they think of interesting questions about your movie-watching behavior." For example, one day the kids wondered about sequels: would a Netflix user who liked the first two "Matrix" movies be just as likely to enjoy the third one, even though it was widely considered to be pretty dreadful?

Each time he or his kids think of a new approach, Bertoni writes a computer program to test it. Each new algorithm takes on average three or four hours to churn through the data on the family's "quad core" Gateway computer. Bertoni's results have gradually improved. When I last spoke to him, he was at No. 8 on the leader board; his program was 8.8 percent better than Cinematch. The top team was at 9.44 percent. Bertoni said he thought he was within striking distance of victory.

But his progress had slowed to a crawl. The more Bertoni improved upon Netflix, the harder it became to move his number forward. This wasn't just his problem, though; the other competitors say that their progress is stalling, too, as they edge toward 10 percent. Why?

Bertoni says it's partly because of "Napoleon Dynamite," an indie comedy from 2004 that achieved cult status and went on to become extremely popular on Netflix. It is, Bertoni and others have discovered, maddeningly hard to determine how much people will like it. When Bertoni runs his algorithms on regular hits like "Lethal Weapon" or

"Miss Congeniality" and tries to predict how any given Netflix user will rate them, he's usually within eight-tenths of a star. But with films like "Napoleon Dynamite," he's off by an average of 1.2 stars.

The reason, Bertoni says, is that "Napoleon Dynamite" is very weird and very polarizing. It contains a lot of arch, ironic humor, including a famously kooky dance performed by the titular teenage character to help his hapless friend win a student-council election. It's the type of quirky entertainment that tends to be either loved or despised. The movie has been rated more than two million times in the Netflix database, and the ratings are disproportionately one or five stars.

Worse, close friends who normally share similar film aesthetics often heatedly disagree about whether "Napoleon Dynamite" is a masterpiece or an annoying bit of hipster self-indulgence. When Bertoni saw the movie himself with a group of friends, they argued for hours over it. "Half of them loved it, and half of them hated it," he told me. "And they couldn't really say why. It's just a difficult movie."

Mathematically speaking, "Napoleon Dynamite" is a very significant problem for the Netflix Prize. Amazingly, Bertoni has deduced that this single movie is causing 15 percent of his remaining error rate; or to put it another way, if Bertoni could anticipate whether you'd like "Napoleon Dynamite" as accurately as he can for other movies, this feat alone would bring him 15 percent of the way to winning the $1 million prize. And while "Napoleon Dynamite" is the worst culprit, it isn't the only troublemaker. A small subset of other titles have caused almost as much bedevilment among the Netflix Prize competitors. When Bertoni showed me a list of his 25 most-difficult-to-predict movies, I noticed they were all similar in some way to "Napoleon Dynamite" — culturally or politically polarizing and hard to classify, including "I Heart Huckabees," "Lost in Translation," "Fahrenheit 9/11," "The Life Aquatic With Steve Zissou," "Kill Bill: Volume 1" and "Sideways."

So this is the question that gently haunts the Netflix competition, as well as the recommendation engines used by other online stores like Amazon and iTunes. Just how predictable is human taste, anyway? And if we can't understand our own preferences, can computers really be any better at it?

It used to be that if you wanted to buy a book, rent a movie or shop for some music, you had to rely on flesh-and-blood judgment — yours, or that of someone you trusted. You'd go to your local store and look for new stuff, or you might just wander the aisles in what librarians call a stack search, to see if anything jumped out at you. You might check out newspaper reviews or consult your friends; if you were lucky, your local video store employed one of those young cinéastes who could size you up in a glance and suggest something suitable.

The advent of online retailing completely upended this cultural and economic ecosystem. First of all, shopping over the Web is not a social experience; there are no clever clerks to ask for advice. What's more, because they have no real space constraints, online stores like Amazon or iTunes can stock millions of titles, making a stack search essentially impossible. This creates the classic problem of choice: how do you decide among an effectively infinite number of options?

But Web sites have this significant advantage over brick-and-mortar stores: They can track everything their customers do. Every page you visit, every purchase you make, every item you rate — it is all recorded. In the early '90s, scientists working in the field of "machine learning" realized that this enormous trove of data could be used to analyze patterns in people's taste. In 1994, Pattie Maes, an M.I.T. professor, created one of the first recommendation engines by setting up a Web site where people listed songs and bands they liked. Her computer algorithm performed what's known as collaborative filtering. It would take a song you rated highly, find other people who had also rated it highly and then suggest you try a song that those people also said they liked.

"We had this realization that if we gathered together a really large group of people, like thousands or millions, they could help one another find things, because you can find patterns in what they like," Maes told me recently. "It's not necessarily the one, single smart critic that is going to find something for you, like, 'Go see this movie, go listen to this band!' "

In one sense, collaborative filtering is less personalized than a store clerk. The clerk, in theory anyway, knows a lot about you, like your age and profession and what sort of things you enjoy; she can even read your current mood. (Are you feeling lousy? Maybe it's not the day for "Apocalypse Now.") A collaborative-filtering program, in contrast, knows very little about you — only what you've bought at a Web site and whether you rated it highly or not. But the computer has numbers on its side. It may know only a little bit about you, but it also knows a little bit about a huge number of other people. This lets it detect patterns we often cannot see on our own. For example, Maes's music-recommendation system discovered that people who like classical music also like the Beatles. It is an epiphany that perhaps make sense when you think about it for a second, but it isn't immediately obvious.

Soon after Maes's work made its debut, online stores quickly understood the value of having a recommendation system, and today most Web sites selling entertainment products have one. Most of them use some variant of collaborative filtering — like Amazon's "Customers Who Bought This Item Also Bought" function. Some set-ups ask you to actively rate products, as Netflix does. But others also rely on passive information. They keep track of your everyday behavior, looking for clues to your preferences. (For example, many music-recommendation engines — like the Genius feature on Apple's iTunes, Microsoft's Mixview music recommender or the Audioscrobbler program at Last.fm — can register every time you listen to a song on your computer or MP3 player.) And a few rare services actually pay people to evaluate products; the Pandora music-streaming service has 50 employees who listen to songs and tag them with descriptors — "upbeat," "minor key," "prominent vocal harmonies."

Netflix came late to the party. The company opened for business in 1997, but for the first three years it offered no recommendations. This wasn't such a big problem when Netflix stocked only 1,000 titles or so, because customers could sift through those pretty quickly. But Netflix grew, and today, it stocks more than 100,000 movies. "I think that once you get beyond 1,000 choices, a recommendation system becomes critical," Hastings, the Netflix C.E.O., told me. "People have limited cognitive time they want to spend on picking a movie."

Cinematch was introduced in 2000, but the first version worked poorly — "a mix of insightful and boneheaded recommendations," according to Hastings. His programmers slowly began improving the algorithms. They could tell how much better they were getting by trying to replicate how a customer rated movies in the past. They took the customer's ratings from, say, 2001, and used them to predict their ratings for 2002. Because Netflix actually had those later ratings, it could discern what a "perfect" prediction would look like. Soon, Cinematch reached the point where it could tease out some fairly nuanced — and surprising — connections. For example, it found that people who enjoy "The Patriot" also tend to like "Pearl Harbor," which you'd expect, since they're both history-war-action movies; but it also discovered that they like the heartstring-tugging drama "Pay It Forward" and the sci-fi movie "I, Robot."

Cinematch has, in fact, become a video-store roboclerk: its suggestions now drive a surprising 60 percent of Netflix's rentals. It also often steers a customer's attention away from big-grossing hits toward smaller, independent movies. Traditional video stores depend on hits; just-out-of-the-theaters blockbusters account for 80 percent of what they rent. At Netflix, by contrast, 70 percent of what it sends out is from the backlist — older movies or small, independent ones. A good recommendation system, in other words, does not merely help people find new stuff. As Netflix has discovered, it also spurs them to consume *more* stuff.

For Netflix, this is doubly important. Customers pay a flat monthly rate, generally $16.99 (although cheaper plans are available), to check out as many movies as they want. The problem with this business model is that new members often have a couple of dozen movies in mind that they want to see, but after that they're not sure what to check out next, and their requests slow. And a customer paying $17 a month for only one movie every month or two is at risk of canceling his subscription; the plan makes financial sense, from a user's point of view, only if you rent a lot of movies. (My wife and I once quit Netflix for precisely this reason.) Every time Hastings increases the quality of Cinematch even slightly, it keeps his customers active.

But by 2006, Cinematch's improving performance had plateaued. Netflix's programmers couldn't go any further on their own. They suspected that there was a big breakthrough out there; the science of recommendation systems was booming, and computer scientists were publishing hundreds of papers each year on the subject. At a staff meeting in the summer of 2006, Hastings suggested a radical idea: Why not have a public contest? Netflix's recommendation system was powered by the wisdom of crowds; now it would tap the wisdom of crowds to get better too.

As Hastings hoped, the contest has galvanized nerds around the world. The Top 10 list for the Netflix Prize currently includes a group of programmers in Austria (who are at No. 2), a trained psychologist and Web consultant in Britain who uses his teenage daughter to perform his calculus (No. 9), a lone Ph.D. candidate in Boston who calls himself My Brain and His Chain (a reference to a Ben Folds song; he's at No. 6) and Pragmatic Theory — two French-Canadian guys in Montreal (No. 3). Nearly every team is working on the prize in its spare time. In October, when I dropped by the house of Martin Chabbert, a 32-year-old member of the Pragmatic Theory duo, it was only 8:30 at night, but we had to whisper: his four children, including a 2-month-old baby, had just gone to bed upstairs. In his small dining room, a laptop sat open next to children's books like "Les Robots: Au Service de L'homme" and a "Star Wars" picture book in French.

"This is where I do everything," Chabbert said. "After the kids are asleep and I've packed the lunches for school, I come down at 9 in the evening and work until 11 or 12. It was very exciting in the beginning!" He laughed. "It still is, but with the baby now, going to bed at midnight is not a good idea."

Pragmatic Theory formed last spring, when Chabbert's longtime friend Martin Piotte — a 43-year-old electrical and computer engineer — heard about the Netflix Prize. Like many of the amateurs trying to win the $1 million, they had no relevant expertise. ("Absolutely no background in statistics that was useful," Piotte told me ruefully. "Two guys, absolutely no clue.") But they soon discovered that the Netflix competition is a fairly collegial affair. The company hosts a discussion board devoted to the prize, and competitors frequently help one another out — discussing algorithms they've tried and publicly brainstorming new ways to improve their work, sometimes even posting reams of computer code for anyone to use. When someone makes a breakthrough, pretty soon every other team is aware of it and starts using it, too. Piotte and Chabbert soon learned the major mathematical tricks that had propelled the leading teams into the Top 10.

The first major breakthrough came less than a month into the competition. A team named Simon Funk vaulted from nowhere into the No. 4 position, improving upon Cinematch by 3.88 percent in one fell swoop. Its secret was a mathematical technique called singular value decomposition. It isn't new; mathematicians have used it for years to make sense of prodigious chunks of information. But Netflix never thought to try it on movies.

Singular value decomposition works by uncovering "factors" that Netflix customers like or don't like. Say, for example, that "Sleepless in Seattle" has been rated by 200,000 Netflix users. In one sense, this is just a huge list of numbers — user No. 452 gave it two stars; No. 985 gave it five stars; and so on. But you could also think of those ratings as individual reactions to various aspects of the movie. "Sleepless in Seattle" is a "chick flick," a comedy, a star vehicle for Tom Hanks; each customer is reacting to how much — or how little — he or she likes "chick flicks," comedies and Tom Hanks. Singular value decomposition takes the mass of Netflix data — 17,770 movies, ratings by 480,189 users — and automatically sorts the films. The programmers do not actively tell the computer what to look for; they just run the algorithm until it groups together movies that share qualities with predictive value.

Sometimes when you look at the clusters of movies, you can deduce the connections. Chabbert showed me one list: at the top were "Sleepless in Seattle," "Steel Magnolias" and "Pretty Woman," while at the bottom were "Star Trek" movies. Clearly, the computer recognized some factor that suggests that someone who likes the romantic aspect of "Pretty Woman" will probably like "Sleepless in Seattle" and dislike "Star Trek." Chabbert showed me another cluster: this time DVD collections of the TV show "Friends" all clustered at the top of the list, while action movies like "Reindeer Games" and thrillers like "Hannibal" clustered at the bottom. Most likely, the computer had selected for "comic" content here. Other lists appear to group movies based on whether they lean strongly to the ideological right or left.

As programmers extract more and more values, it becomes possible to draw exceedingly sophisticated correlations among movies and hence to offer incredibly nuanced recommendations. "We're teasing out very subtle human behaviors," said Chris Volinsky, a scientist with AT&T in New Jersey who is one of the most successful Netflix contestants; his three-person team held the No. 1 position for more than a year. His team relies, in part, on singular value decomposition. "You can find things like 'People who like action movies, but only if there's a lot of explosions, and not if there's a lot of blood. And maybe they don't like profanity,' " Volinsky told me when we spoke recently. "Or it's like 'I like action movies, but not if they have Keanu Reeves and not if there's a bus involved.' "

Most of the leading teams competing for the Netflix Prize now use singular value decomposition. Indeed, given how quickly word of new breakthroughs spreads among the competitors, virtually every team in the Top 10 makes use of similar mathematical ploys. The only thing that separates their scores is how skillfully they tweak their algorithms. The Netflix Prize has come to resemble a drag race in which everyone drives the same car, with only tiny modifications to the fuel injection.

Yet those tweaks are crucial. Since the top teams are so close — there is less than a tenth of a percent between each contender — even tiny improvements can boost a team to the top of the charts.

These days, the competitors spend much of their time thinking deeply about the math and psychology behind recommendations. For example, the teams are grappling with the problem that over time, people can change how sternly or leniently they rate movies. Psychological studies show that if you ask someone to rate a movie and then, a month later, ask him to do so again, the rating varies by an average of 0.4 stars. "The question is why," Len Bertoni said to me. "Did you just remember it differently? Did you see something in between? Did something change in your life that made you rethink it?" Some teams deal with this by programming their computers to gradually discount older ratings.

Another common problem is identifying overly punitive raters. If you're a really harsh critic and I'm a much more easygoing one, your two-star rating may be equal to my four-star rating. To compensate, an algorithm might try to detect when a Netflix customer tends to hand out only one- or two-star ratings — a sign of a strict, pursed-lip customer — and artificially boost his or her ratings by a half-star or so. Then there's the problem of movie raters who simply aren't consistent. They might be evenhanded most of the time, but if they log into Netflix when they're in a particularly bad mood, they might impulsively decide to rate a couple of dozen movies harshly.

TV shows, which are hot commodities on Netflix, present yet another perplexing issue. Customers respond to TV series much differently than they do to movies. People who loved the first two seasons of "The Wire" might start getting bored during the third but keep on watching for a while, then stop abruptly. So when should Cinematch stop recommending "The Wire"? When do you tell someone to give up on a TV show?

Interestingly, the Netflix Prize competitors do not know anything about the demographics of the customers whose taste they're trying to predict. The teams sometimes argue on the discussion board about whether their predictions would be better if they knew that customer

No. 465 is, for example, a 23-year-old woman in Arizona. Yet most of the leading teams say that personal information is not very useful, because it's too crude. As one team pointed out to me, the fact that I'm a 40-year-old West Village resident is not very predictive. There's little reason to think the other 40-year-old men on my block enjoy the same movies as I do. In contrast, the Netflix data are much more rich in meaning. When I tell Netflix that I think Woody Allen's black comedy "Match Point" deserves three stars but the Joss Whedon sci-fi film "Serenity" is a five-star masterpiece, this reveals quite a lot about my taste. Indeed, Reed Hastings told me that even though Netflix has a good deal of demographic information about its users, the company does not currently use it much to generate movie recommendations; merely knowing who people are, paradoxically, isn't very predictive of their movie tastes.

As the teams have grown better at predicting human preferences, the more incomprehensible their computer programs have become, even to their creators. Each team has lined up a gantlet of scores of algorithms, each one analyzing a slightly different correlation between movies and users. The upshot is that while the teams are producing ever-more-accurate recommendations, they cannot precisely explain how they're doing this. Chris Volinsky admits that his team's program has become a black box, its internal logic unknowable.

There's a sort of unsettling, alien quality to their computers' results. When the teams examine the ways that singular value decomposition is slotting movies into categories, sometimes it makes sense to them — as when the computer highlights what appears to be some essence of nerdiness in a bunch of sci-fi movies. But many categorizations are now so obscure that they cannot see the reasoning behind them. Possibly the algorithms are finding connections so deep and subconscious that customers themselves wouldn't even recognize them. At one point, Chabbert showed me a list of movies that his algorithm had discovered share some ineffable similarity; it includes a historical movie, "Joan of Arc," a wrestling video, "W.W.E.: SummerSlam 2004," the comedy "It Had to Be You" and a version of Charles Dickens's "Bleak House." For the life of me, I can't figure out what possible connection they have, but Chabbert assures me that this singular value decomposition scored 4 percent higher than Cinematch — so it must be doing something right. As Volinsky surmised, "They're able to tease out all of these things that we would never, ever think of ourselves." The machine may be understanding something about us that we do not understand ourselves.

Yet it's clear that something is still missing. Volinsky's momentum has slowed down significantly, as everyone else's has. There's some X factor in human judgment that the current bunch of algorithms isn't capturing when it comes to movies like "Napoleon Dynamite." And the problem looms large. Bertoni is currently at 8.8 percent; he says that a small group of mainly independent movies represents more than half of the remaining errors in the way of winning the prize. Most teams suspect that continuing to tweak existing algorithms won't be enough to get to 10 percent. They need another breakthrough — some way to digitally replicate the love/hate dynamic that governs hard-to-pigeonhole indie films.

"This last half-percent really is the Mount Everest," Volinsky said. "It's going to take one of these 'aha' moments."

Some computer scientists think the "Napoleon Dynamite" problem exposes a serious weakness of computers. They cannot anticipate the eccentric ways that real people actually decide to take a chance on a movie.

The Cinematch system, like any recommendation engine, assumes that your taste is static and unchanging. The computer looks at all the movies you've rated in the past, finds the trend and uses that to guide you. But the reality is that our cultural tastes evolve, and they change in part because we interact with others. You hear your friends gushing about "Mad Men," so eventually — even though you have never had any particular interest in early-'60s America — you give it a try. Or you go into the video store and run into a particularly charismatic clerk who persuades you that you really, really have to give "The Life Aquatic With Steve Zissou" a chance.

As Gavin Potter, a Netflix Prize competitor who lives in Britain and is currently in ninth place, pointed out to me, a computerized recommendation system seeks to find the common threads in millions of people's recommendations, so it inherently avoids extremes. Video-store clerks, on the other hand, are influenced by their own idiosyncrasies. Even if they're considering your taste to make a suitable recommendation, they can't help relying on their own sense of what's good and bad. They'll make more mistakes than the Netflix computers — but they're also more likely to have flashes of inspiration, like pointing you to "Napoleon Dynamite" at just the right moment.

"If you use a computerized system based on ratings, you will tend to get very relevant but safe answers," Potter says. "If you go with the movie-store clerk, you will get more unpredictable but potentially more exciting recommendations."

Another critic of computer recommendations is, oddly enough, Pattie Maes, the M.I.T. professor. She notes that there's something slightly anti-social — "narrow-minded" — about hyperpersonalized recommendation systems. Sure, it's good to have a computer find more of what you already like. But culture isn't experienced in solitude. We also consume shows and movies and music as a way of participating in society. That social need can override the question of whether or not we'll like the movie.

"You don't want to see a movie just because you think it's going to be good," Maes says. "It's also because everyone at school or work is going to be talking about it, and you want to be able to talk about it, too." Maes told me that a while ago she rented a "Sex and the City" DVD from Netflix. She suspected she probably wouldn't really like the show. "But everybody else was constantly talking about it, and I had to know what they were talking about," she says. "So even though I would have been embarrassed if Netflix suggested 'Sex and the City' to me, I'm glad I saw it, because now I get it. I know all the in-jokes."

Maes suspects that in the future, computer-based reasoning will become less important for online retailers than social-networking tools that tap into the social zeitgeist, that let customers see, in Facebook fashion, for example, what their close friends are watching and buying.

(Potter has an even more intriguing idea. He says he thinks that a recommendation system could predict cultural microtrends by monitoring news events. His research has found, for example, that people rent more movies about Wall Street when the stock market drops.) In the world of music, there are already several innovative recommendation services that try to analyze buzz — by monitoring blogs for repeated mentions of up-and-coming bands, or by sifting through millions of people's playlists to see if a new band is suddenly getting a lot of attention.

Of course, for a company like Netflix, there's a downside to pushing exciting-but-risky movie recommendations on viewers. If Netflix tries to stretch your taste by recommending more daring movies, it also risks annoying customers. A bad movie recommendation can waste an evening.

Is there any way to find a golden mean? When I put the question to Reed Hastings, the Netflix C.E.O., he told me he suspects that there won't be any simple answer. The company needs better algorithms; it needs breakthrough techniques like singular value decomposition, with the brilliant but inscrutable insights it enables. But Hastings also says he thinks Maes is right, too, and that social-networking tools will become more useful. (Netflix already has one, in fact — an application that lets users see what their family and peers are renting. But Hastings admits it hasn't been as valuable as computerized intelligence; only a very small percentage of rentals are driven by what friends have chosen.) Hastings is even considering hiring cinephiles to watch all 100,000 movies in the Netflix library and write up, by hand, pages of adjectives describing each movie, a cloud of tags that would offer a subjective view of what makes films similar or dissimilar. It might imbue Cinematch with more unpredictable, humanlike intelligence.

"Human beings are very quirky and individualistic, and wonderfully idiosyncratic," Hastings says. "And while I love that about human beings, it makes it hard to figure out what they like."

CLIVE THOMPSON, a contributing writer for The New York Times Magazine, writes frequently about technology.

The Google Algorithm

EDITORIAL | BY THE NEW YORK TIMES | JULY 14, 2010

GOOGLE HANDLES NEARLY two-thirds of Internet search queries world-wide. Analysts reckon that most Web sites rely on the search engine for half of their traffic. When Google engineers tweak its supersecret algorithm — as they do hundreds of times a year — they can break the business of a Web site that is pushed down the rankings.

When Google was a pure search engine, it was easy to appear agnostic about search results, with no reason to play favorites with one Web site or another. But as Google has branched out into online services from maps and videos to comparison shopping, it has acquired pecuniary incentives to favor its own over rivals.

Google argues that its behavior is kept in check by competitors like Yahoo or Bing. But Google has become the default search engine for many Internet users. Competitors are a click away, but a case is building for some sort of oversight of the gatekeeper of the Internet.

In the past few months, Google has come under investigation by antitrust regulators in Europe. Rivals have accused Google of placing the Web sites of affiliates like Google Maps or YouTube at the top of Internet searches and relegating competitors to obscurity down the list. In the United States, Google said it expects antitrust regulators to scrutinize its $700 million purchase of the flight information software firm ITA, with which it plans to enter the online travel search market occupied by Expedia, Orbitz, Bing and others.

The accusations in Europe may or may not have merit. Google says it only tweaks its algorithm to improve its searches. Some Web sites that have accused Google of unfair placing are merely collections of links with next to no original content of their own, precisely the kind of sites that Google's search algorithm screens out to better answer queries. Antitrust regulators in the United States could well let Google buy ITA because it does not now provide online travel services.

Still, the potential impact of Google's algorithm on the Internet economy is such that it is worth exploring ways to ensure that the editorial policy guiding Google's tweaks is solely intended to improve the quality of the results and not to help Google's other businesses.

Some early suggestions for how to accomplish this include having Google explain with some specified level of detail the editorial policy that guides its tweaks. Another would be to give some government commission the power to look at those tweaks.

Google provides an incredibly valuable service, and the government must be careful not to stifle its ability to innovate. Forcing it to publish the algorithm or the method it uses to evaluate it would allow every Web site to game the rules in order to climb up the rankings — destroying its value as a search engine. Requiring each algorithm tweak to be approved by regulators could drastically slow down its improvements. Forbidding Google to favor its own services — such as when it offers a Google Map to queries about addresses — might reduce the value of its searches.

With these caveats in mind, if Google is to continue to be the main map to the information highway, it concerns us all that it leads us fairly to where we want to go.

CHAPTER 2

Clickbait and Sponsored Content Change Media

As content began to "go viral" on social media, advertisers and media companies took notice. Many websites, earning ad revenue for every click, wrote provocative "clickbait" style headlines that promised more than the articles delivered. "Native" content, produced by advertisers, blurred the line between content and advertising. Journalism as "content" fostered legitimate news sources, alongside often bizarre streams of junk articles. The fate of these publishers was often shaped by the Facebook news feed, whose algorithms could direct the attention of millions of readers.

Risks Abound as Reporters Play in Traffic

COLUMN | BY DAVID CARR | MARCH 23, 2014

IT IS A DIRTY SECRET of the journalism profession that many reporters are bad at math. Many of us ended up typing our way to a living because we had an easier time making words dance than numbers.

But now that everything can be measured, we have to keep an eye on both. Journalists who were paid to write when the muse or events beckoned, are now held accountable for the amount of work they produce and the volume of traffic it attracts.

Gee, it's almost like news is supposed to be a business or something.

The availability of ready metrics on content is not only changing the way news organizations compensate their employees, but will have a significant effect on the news itself.

If I were being paid by the click for this column, I might have begun it this way: Will an oppressive emphasis on "click bait" mean that the news ends up imprisoned by transgendered models posing in disgraceful listicles accompanied by kidnapped nude kittens?

But I'm not. So let's just say that there is a growing trend in many corners of journalism to tie the compensation of journalists to the amount of web traffic and/or articles they generate.

At the beginning of the month, TheStreet.com, a site that covers the stock market, announced it was expanding its platform to include new voices, and that contributors would be paid by the click. A contributor who receives 60,000 page views in a week, for example, would be paid $50. (A lot of mischief can occur when stock prices are being written about, but we'll get back to that later.)

At the end of February, The Daily Caller, a conservative political site run by Tucker Carlson, said it would begin a hybrid arrangement in which staff writers were paid a base salary plus a traffic incentive. The Daily Caller's publisher told The Washington Post that the new plan would lead to more traffic and higher overall compensation for writers.

Joel Johnson, the editorial director of Gawker Media, announced a program in February called "Recruits" that creates subsidiary sites for new contributors, attached to existing editorial sites like Gawker or Jezebel. The recruits receive a stipend of $1,500 a month, and pay back that amount at a rate of $5 for every 1,000 unique visitors they attract. They then get to keep anything above the amount of the stipend, up to $6,000.

At the end of 90 days, the contributors are evaluated and retained or cut loose based on their traffic performance. (Gawker has long been a pioneer in traffic transparency and giving its writers bonuses based on traction in the marketplace.)

Depending on your perspective, the trend could be a long overdue embrace of the realities of the publishing landscape, or one more step down the road to perdition. Nick Denton, the founder of Gawker, is bullish on the effect of new pay paradigms.

"The journalist will do extremely well in the next 10 years. It will be a booming profession," he said, adding that he agreed with a recent suggestion by the venture capitalist Marc Andreessen that "news will be 10 times the size it was."

Others worry that compensation built on metrics will leave working journalists on the short end of the stick.

"It is very early days of pay-for-click for professional writers," said Minda Zetlin, president of the American Society of Journalists and Authors and a columnist for Inc.'s website. "In terms of it being a bonanza for writers, that is far from true right now, but there will be value in learning best practices and where our traffic comes from."

It's not just digital upstarts that are starting to manage reporters by the numbers. The Portland, Ore., newspaper The Oregonian, the much heralded home of many Pulitzer Prize-winning projects, is in the midst of a reorganization driven by the desire for more web traffic, according to internal documents obtained by Willamette Week, a weekly newspaper in Portland. A year after big layoffs and a reduction in home delivery to four times a week, The Oregonian, owned by Newhouse's Advance Publications, is focusing on digital journalism — and the people who produce it — with a great deal of specificity.

Beginning immediately, according to the documents, the company's leadership will require reporters to post new articles three times a day, and to post the first comment under any significant article. It's part of a companywide initiative to increase page views by 27.7 percent in the coming year. Beyond that, reporters are expected to increase their average number of daily posts by 25 percent by the middle of the year and an additional 15 percent in the second half of the year.

If that sounds like it won't leave much time for serious work, the new initiative also calls for reporters to "produce top-flight journalistic and digitally oriented enterprise as measured by two major projects a quarter," which will include "goals by projects on page views and engagement." In the more-with-less annals of corporate mandates, this one is a doozy. Contacted by email, Peter Bhatia, who is departing as editor of The Oregonian, scheduled an interview, but then declined to comment.

The emphasis on page views and productivity in both old media and new is turning heads among people who study the news business, including Nikki Usher, an assistant professor at George Washington University's school of media and public affairs.

"Reporters have always been incentivized for doing big, popular news in terms of internal recognition, but I think it is revolutionary for traditional news organizations to follow the dictates of traffic," she said. "On some level, they are coming clean, owning up to the fundamental realities that there are going to be significant changes to the business model."

For people who grew up in a digital news environment, the emphasis on traffic is not very much of a shock.

"Historically, writers never got to participate in the success if they came up with something that is truly viral, so it sort of makes sense that they might end up getting paid more for something that is massively successful," said Choire Sicha, founder of The Awl, a website focused on culture and current events. The Awl doesn't pay by the click, but does occasionally pay a bonus for a big win by a writer, as it did for a recent popular post about life on the other side of the coffee shop counter.

And journalism's status as a profession is up for grabs. A viral hit is no longer defined by the credentials of an individual or organization. The media ecosystem is increasingly a pro-am affair, where the wisdom — or prurient interest — of the crowd decides what is important and worthy of sharing.

Gawker Media now hosts Kinja, a platform where anybody can publish a blog post. The leader board on Kinja is a mix of people who write for a living, and people who wrote something about living that connected with other people.

It's bracingly meritocratic, but there are hazards. Quizzes are everywhere right now because readers can't resist clicking on them, but on an informational level, they are mostly empty calories. There are any number of gambits to induce clicks, from LOL cats to slide shows to bait-and-switch headlines.

But more than just traffic can be manipulated once you open up the gates, as Fortune recently pointed out. Authors promoting specific stocks posted to sites — including Forbes.com, Seeking Alpha, and Wall St. Cheat Sheet — without disclosing that they were paid to promote the companies they were writing about. The stocks were pumped and sometimes dumped without the reader being any the wiser.

Now that metrics are part of the news agenda, all of the sticks are in the air. Just because something is popular does not make it worthy, but ignoring audience engagement is a sure route to irrelevance. I'm happy to let the things I write stand on their own merit.

The Media Equation is a column from **DAVID CARR** focused on the intersection of media and technology.

Arianna Huffington's Improbable, Insatiable Content Machine

BY DAVID SEGAL | JUNE 30, 2015

She did more than anyone else to invent the Internet news business. After a decade, despite setbacks, she is still setting the pace.

ONE MORNING IN MARCH, a dozen Huffington Post staff members gathered around a glass table in Arianna Huffington's office. They had been summoned to deliver a progress report to Huffington, the site's president, editor in chief and co-founder, on a new initiative, What's Working. It was created to help the site cover solutions, rather than focusing only on the world's problems — or as Huffington explained in an internal memo in January, to "start a positive contagion by relentlessly telling the stories of people and communities doing amazing things, overcoming great odds and facing real challenges with perseverance, creativity and grace."

Huffington, who is 64, was getting over a cold, and coughed hoarsely now and then. She sipped a soy cappuccino through a straw as she asked for updates in her purring, singsongy Greek accent. One by one, staff members went through their story lists: corporations with innovative plans to reduce water use, a nonprofit putting former gang members to work, Muslims confronting radicalism. Huffington kept the pace brisk; she sounded like a person in a hurry trying hard to not sound like one. When an editor hashed out ways to present a new, recurring feature called the What's Working Media Honor Roll — a roundup of similarly positive journalism from other publications — she suggested that he launch first and tinker later.

"I think let's start iterating," she said. "Let's not wait for the perfect product."

What's Working might sound like a significant departure for a site that, like most media outlets, thrives on tales of conflict and wrongdoing.

DAVE KOTINSKY/GETTY IMAGES

Arianna Huffington at the AOL BUILD Speaker Series earlier this month.

But in a sense What's Working is not a departure at all. The Huffington Post has always been guided by the question: What works? Namely, what draws traffic? The answer has changed constantly. When Huffington co-founded the site in 2005, Facebook was still just a network for college students. Today, roughly half her mobile traffic comes from social media, Facebook above all. Arguably, this shift in browsing habits, as much as Huffington's distaste for the media's built-in bias toward negativity, helped inspire What's Working. The initiative is in part an effort to get readers to share more Huffington Post stories on Facebook.

"The numbers are amazing," Huffington said as staff members filed out. "You're not as likely to share a story of a beheading. Right? I mean, you'll read it."

Within The Huffington Post, and away from the glass table, some staff members have fretted that What's Working could result in a steady drip of pallid, upbeat stories (e.g., "How Hugh Jackman's Coffee Brand Is Changing Lives"). But it's hard to argue with Huffington's intuitions when it comes to generating traffic. Her site has more than 200 million unique visitors each month, according to comScore, and it is one of the country's top online destinations for news.

Nevertheless, in May, Huffington's tenure as editor in chief was briefly in question. The site's corporate parent, AOL, was sold to Verizon for $4.4 billion, and Huffington was forced to spend a few weeks negotiating the terms of the site's future with her new overlords. During that process, AOL revealed that two suitors, earlier in the year, tried to buy The Huffington Post for $1 billion, or roughly four times what Jeff Bezos paid for The Washington Post two years ago. Plainly, to certain investors, digital media companies are valuable because they deliver enormous audiences. Any difficulty turning a profit — The Huffington Post broke even last year on $146 million in revenue, according to someone familiar with the site's finances — is considered a temporary problem that will eventually be fixed by the sheer size of the readership.

This singular focus on audience development expresses itself in different ways at different publications. At The Huffington Post, it takes the shape of an editorial mandate that, much like the universe itself, is unfathomably broad and constantly expanding. At least in theory, nothing gets past its editors and writers. They cover, in most cases through aggregation, everything from Federal Reserve policy to celebrity antics, from Islamic State atrocities to parenting tips, supplemented with a steady stream of uncategorizable click bait ("Can Cannibalism Fight Brain Disease? Only Sort Of").

To work at The Huffington Post is to run a race without a finish line, at a clip that is forever quickening. The pace is stressful for many employees, who describe a newsroom with plenty of turnover. One former staff member I spoke with, who developed an ulcer while working there, called The Huffington Post "a jury-rigged, discombobulated chaos machine."

Huffington may be the Internet's most improbable media pioneer. This is her first job as an editor or publisher, and few would describe her as a techie. But as one of the first major media properties born in the full light of the digital age, The Huffington Post has always been a skunk works for the sorts of experiments that have come to define the news business in the Internet era.

In its early days, when most visits came through Google searches, the site mastered search-engine optimization (S.E.O.), the art of writing stories based on topics trending on Google and larding headlines with keywords. The site's annual "What Time Is the Super Bowl?" post has become such a famous example of S.E.O.-driven non-news that other media outlets have written half-disgusted, half-admiring posts dissecting its history.

When most sites were merely guessing about what would resonate with readers, The Huffington Post brought a radical data-driven methodology to its home page, automatically moving popular stories to more prominent spaces and A-B testing its headlines. The site's editorial director, Danny Shea, demonstrated to me how this works a few months ago, opening an online dashboard and pulling up an article about General Motors. One headline was "How GM Silenced a Whistleblower." Another read "How GM Bullied a Whistleblower." The site had automatically shown different headlines to different readers and found that "Silence" was outperforming "Bully." So "Silence" it would be. It's this sort of obsessive data analysis that has helped web-headline writing become so viscerally effective.

Above all, from its founding in an era dominated by "web magazines" like Slate, The Huffington Post has demonstrated the value of quantity. Early in its history, the site increased its breadth on the cheap by hiring young writers to quickly summarize stories that had been reported by other publications, marking the birth of industrial aggregation.

Today, The Huffington Post employs an armada of young editors, writers and video producers: 850 in all, many toiling at an exhausting pace. It publishes 13 editions across the globe, including sites in India, Germany and Brazil. Its properties collectively push out about 1,900 posts per day. In 2013, Digiday estimated that BuzzFeed, by contrast, was putting out 373 posts per day, The Times 350 per day and Slate

60 per day. (At the time, The Huffington Post was publishing 1,200 posts per day.) Four more editions are in the works — The Huffington Post China among them — and a franchising model will soon take the brand to small and midsize markets, according to an internal memo Huffington sent in late May.

Throughout its history, the site's scale has also depended on free labor. One of Huffington's most important insights early on was that if you provide bloggers with a big enough stage, you don't have to pay them. This audience-for-content trade has been imitated successfully by outlets like Thought Catalog and Bleacher Report, a sports-news website that Turner Broadcasting bought in 2012 for somewhere between $150 million and $200 million.

As this more-is-better ethos has come to define the industry, shifts in online advertising have begun to favor publications that already attract large audiences. Display advertising — wherein advertisers pay each time an ad is shown to a reader — still dominates the market. But native advertising, designed to match the look and feel of the editorial content it runs alongside, has been on the rise for years. BuzzFeed, the media company started in 2006 by Jonah Peretti, a co-founder of The Huffington Post, was built to rely entirely on native advertising. The Huffington Post offers to make its advertisers custom quizzes, listicles, slide shows, videos, infographics, feature articles and blog posts. Prices start at $130,000 for three pieces of content. This is where size matters; top-tier sites can fetch premium rates because advertisers know their messages could be seen by millions. There have been concerns that readers might be deceived by native ads if they are not properly identified — The Huffington Post always clearly labels its sponsored content — but the ethical debate in the media world is over. Socintel360, a research firm, predicts that spending on native advertising in the United States will more than double in the next four years to $18.4 billion.

Kenneth Lerer, another Huffington Post co-founder, believes that news start-ups today are like cable-television networks in the early '80s: small, pioneering companies that will be handsomely rewarded for figuring out how to monetize your attention through a new medium. If this is so, the size of The Huffington Post's audience could one day justify that $1 billion valuation. But at least in cable, the ratings-driven mania of sweeps week comes only four times a year.

Even as she oversees an international news operation, Huffington spends most of her days and nights in a globe-spanning run of lectures, parties, talk shows, conferences and meetings, a never-ending tour that she chronicles in a dizzying Instagram feed. Her stamina is a source of awe to members of what she calls her A-Team — the A is for Arianna — a group of 9 or so Huffington Post staff members who, in addition to their editorial duties, help keep her in perpetual motion. Within the organization, A-Team jobs are known to be all-consuming — but also, for those who last, a ticket to promotion later on. While some stick around for years, many A-Teamers endure only about 12 months before calling it quits or asking to be transferred.

The first time I saw Huffington's unremitting style up close was in New Haven last year, at the start of a tour to promote her self-help book, "Thrive." In all of our interviews, she was warm and entertaining. She has a politician's gift for seeming sincerely interested, having learned that nothing is so disarming as asking personal questions and then listening. She also has a comic's timing. At a Barnes & Noble onstage chat in Manhattan, shortly before the trip to New Haven, the moderator, Katie Couric, asked her who was to blame for the merciless pace of life in corporate America. Huffington paused for a moment. Then she turned to the audience.

"Men," she deadpanned.

In her talk, she described her own transformation from fast-lane addict to evangelist for reflection, sleep and "digital detoxing" — basically, turning off your smartphone whenever possible. This is a catechism she has branded the "third metric" of success, with money and power being the first two. Her conversion narrative begins on the morning of April 6, 2007, when she collapsed from exhaustion. She fell to the floor in her home office, hitting her face on her desk and breaking her cheekbone. Medical tests found nothing that could explain the episode. Huffington realized that her lifestyle, which at the time was filled with 18-hour workdays, seven days a week, was wrecking her health.

"By any sane definition of success," she told the crowd that day in New Haven, "if you are lying in your office in a pool of blood, you are not a success."

The speech, which I caught a few times, is always a hit. Huffington presents herself as a redemption story, someone who overdosed on her mobile phone and survived to warn others. She looks the part, too: a Dolce & Gabbana-ed woman of a certain age, perfectly at ease, regularly brushing back a forelock of honey-blond hair with her fingers. After the speech in New Haven, people lined up to have their copies of "Thrive" signed. One by one, they offered Huffington variations of, "You are an inspiration." Some shared their own success stories.

One woman told her: "In the horse world, I do holistic care, and I'm embarking on a barn that's cutting-edge. It's all about positive reinforcement."

"We'd love you to write about it!" Huffington exclaimed.

Five years ago, in 2010, the site was successful, attracting nearly 25 million unique visitors a month, but it lacked the money Huffington felt it needed to expand. So it seemed fortunate when, later that year, she met Tim Armstrong, chief executive of AOL, at a media conference in New York.

"He asked to meet with me privately, and he said: 'What do you want to do with The Huffington Post?'" Huffington recalled. "And I said, 'I want to be a global company, I want us to be everywhere in the world.'"

Armstrong offered $315 million, and on Feb. 7, 2011, AOL announced the acquisition. Huffington was made the head of the Huffington Post Media Group, an entity that would control AOL's empire of content — an odd mixture of offerings including Moviefone, TechCrunch, Engadget, MapQuest, Autoblog, AOL Music and the collection of hundreds of hyperlocal websites called Patch. In a stroke, Huffington found herself overseeing a diverse portfolio with 117 million unique visitors per month in the United States and 270 million around the world. She also managed several thousand editors, writers, bloggers and business staff members.

Initially, Armstrong and Huffington seemed like a natural match. Each is a fan of big ideas that can be executed quickly; each prizes boldness and energy. At one AOL meeting with brand managers, Armstrong ribbed his underlings by recounting how Huffington called him on a Sunday to tell him what was wrong with AOL's home page. Why had no one else done that?

Integrating a group of such varied websites and personnel would have posed a challenge to any manager. For one who admits to having little interest in organization and planning, it was impossible. Huffington preferred to improvise, and she did so aggressively — "like a hockey player," as one former AOL executive put it, with some admiration.

A clash of cultures, however, was soon evident. Many of AOL's sites did little more than promote their sponsors; AOL Real Estate, for instance, was mainly a home for Bank of America ads, next to stories about the joys of mortgage refinancing. In an attempt to restore some semblance of editorial integrity, Huffington fired the freelancers who worked for the site and replaced them with young staff members. Many were recent graduates of Yale — her feeder of choice — whose chief qualification, aside from the obvious, was a willingness to work for a pittance. But the hiring spree was rushed and filled the sites with fledglings. Page views plunged, irking corporate sponsors.

At first, many on Armstrong's team had been awed by her energy and range, but they quickly grasped that these didn't always translate into results. "No one else could give a commencement speech at Smith one day, meet the prime minister of Japan on Tuesday and debate the Middle East on MSNBC on Wednesday," one former executive said. "But that doesn't mean she knows the ins and outs of running Moviefone." It didn't help that AOL stock, following the acquisition, had fallen to less than $12 by August from just above $20 at the time of the purchase half a year earlier. At some point, Huffington stopped going to meetings of AOL executives, and in April 2012, an organizational reshuffling quietly moved every AOL site except The Huffington Post out of Huffington's portfolio. Her tenure as AOL content czar was over.

By then, Huffington was having a serious case of seller's remorse. During a tech conference, she was overheard at a bar in Rancho Palos Verdes, Calif., talking to the venture capitalist Scott Stanford, then a Goldman Sachs banker. Speaking in a voice loud enough for many to hear, she posed questions like, "Who would buy The Huffington Post?" and "How much would it fetch?" Around that time, Huffington Post employees recall, she went on trips with very rich people and returned with news that the site was about to be purchased again, this time for $1 billion.

But The Huffington Post was no longer Huffington's to sell, and AOL seemed uninterested in parting with it. By October 2012, discontent with Huffington was widespread enough that top executives at AOL were quietly strategizing about ways to ease her into a kind of ceremonial role — one in which she would only promote the site rather than running its day-to-day operations. (A source said the effort was given a one-word shorthand: "Popemobile." Like the Pope in his bulletproof bubble, Huffington would glide through the world and wave.) The idea never caught on, mostly because it was clear Huffington would never agree to it, and by May of this year, when Verizon announced its acquisition of AOL, it had long been abandoned.

Verizon went after AOL principally for its ad-buying technologies, but in mid-June, Verizon's C.E.O. and chairman, Lowell McAdam, said he was committed to keeping The Huffington Post, as incidental as its acquisition may have been. Huffington, whose contract with AOL expired earlier in the year, wanted guarantees that Verizon would finance the site's growth and keep its hands off articles with which it may have a difference of opinion — those on net neutrality, for instance.

Soon after the Verizon-AOL deal was announced, Huffington began to negotiate her future and the future of The Huffington Post. According to two sources, Armstrong suggested closing the acquisition first and prodding Verizon to make promises about The Huffington Post later. Huffington refused, and she held out until mid-June, when Verizon pledged more than $100 million a year for ongoing operations and vowed to give the site editorial autonomy. (Others with knowledge of the talks say that no financial commitments have been made yet.) The money will allow The Huffington Post to broaden its video offerings, supporting a 24-hour online network and what Huffington called, in an internal memo, a "rapid-response satire unit." Assurances in hand, Huffington signed a new four-year contract that will keep her in situ as editor in chief.

None of this necessarily means that The Huffington Post will remain in Verizon's permanent portfolio. In fact, if Verizon's real goal is to offload the site, it has done exactly what it should to burnish the asset for eventual sale. Were suitors to come courting again, they would surely offer less for a Huffington-less Huffington Post.

That is not to say that Huffington is inexpensive to keep around. She flies all around the planet, occasionally with members of the A-Team in tow. A-Team duties include tending to Huffington's Twitter account, her Instagram feed and her Facebook posts; running her errands; organizing her day; planning her travel; and prepping her speeches, which, if they aren't pro bono, cost at least $100,000. One former A-Teamer recalled loading The Huffington Post on Huffington's computer when she showed up at the office.

"Arianna doesn't surf the web," the former A-Teamer explained. "She reads stories that people send on her iPhone, and she sends and receives emails on her BlackBerry. But I've never seen her on a computer, surfing the web." Huffington said that this is not true, and stated that she ditched her BlackBerry nearly two years ago. But more than a dozen former and current Huffington Post staff members said they had never seen her so much as open a web browser.

Some former employees file this in the category, Things at Odds With Arianna's Public Image. Also in this category is the vibe at The Huffington Post's downtown Manhattan office. Despite its nap rooms, meditation rooms and breathing classes, which were introduced as Huffington entered her "Thrive" phase, it is described as a surpassingly difficult place to work.

Much of this difficulty is inherent to life at an Internet news site, where victory means beating the competition by a matter of seconds with a post that might yield gobs of traffic. This is why so many editors and writers at The Huffington Post remain at their desks during lunch and keep an eye on the web at all times. If, while you're offline, three new Instagram filters are announced and you're late to post the news, that's a problem. "Just about everyone works continuously, whether you're at the office or not," one former employee said. "That little green light that says you're available on Gchat is what matters."

Low pay worsens the strain. One former employee said that some staff members take second jobs to cover their expenses. Some tutor; others wait on tables; others babysit. (A representative for The Huffington Post said the company was unaware of any moonlighting.) Many staff members rely on what has been called "HuffPost lunch" — Luna Bars, carrots, hummus, apples, bananas and sometimes string cheese, all served gratis in a kitchen area of the office.

Inevitably, there is burnout. At the New York office, nearly two dozen employees have left since the start of this year, either because they were laid off or found more enticing and less hectic jobs. A Gawker post in early June, written by an anonymous former staff member, said the recent departures were hardly a surprise because the place has long been "so brutal and toxic it would meet with approval from committed sociopaths."

A former editor told me about a period in 2013 when a series of departures left a cluster of empty desks along a wall that Huffington walks past on the way to her office. "Someone told my manager, 'Arianna is really stressed out about the number of people leaving, so we need a bunch of people to sit at those desks in the path from the elevator to her office, to make her feel better,' " the former editor said. "So we sat there, waiting to say: 'Hello! Greetings!' as she walked by. It was supposed to be for two hours, but she got there at about 3 in the afternoon instead of 11 in the morning. It was absurd. I had to interrupt my workday because this woman was stressed out, because so many people had left, because they were stressed out." (A Huffington Post representative denied this story, saying it was "clearly made up by someone with an ax to grind.")

Staff members in Huffington's inner circle must also contend with her superhuman endurance. Her oft-repeated claim to sleep eight hours a night notwithstanding, she rarely seems to be idle. Emails from her cease, several ex-employees told me, only between 1 a.m. and 5 a.m.

There are staff members who have stuck it out for years and speak highly of the site as a place to work. They say they form lasting bonds with co-workers and relish the sense that they are writing for millions of readers. Some, like Daniel Koh, a former A-Teamer, speak with a reverence and fondness for Huffington herself. Koh described her as a perfectionist of exceptional intellectual wattage, a leader who never raises her voice and never holds a grudge. "Was it intense, and long hours, and did she teach me to maximize my workday?" he said. "Absolutely."

But others who have worked closely with Huffington have found it a bruising experience, saying that she is perpetually on the lookout for signs of disloyalty, to a degree that bespeaks paranoia or, at the very least, pettiness. Employees cycle in and out of her favor, hailed as the site's savior one moment, ignored the next. (The Gawker post called the office "essentially Soviet in its functioning.") "Everyone's stock is shooting up or falling at any given moment, so everyone is rattled with uncertainty and insecurity," one former employee said. "I've never seen anything like it."

When I asked Huffington about criticisms of the newsroom, she was unmoved. She pointed to the nap rooms and breathing classes as evidence that she took employee well-being seriously. Only the voices of current employees were worth listening to, she cautioned, because the opinions of people who were laid off or left were likely to skew negative. I noted that she seemed unwilling to accept any responsibility for what a lot of former employees said was a vexing atmosphere.

"I'm definitely a work in progress," she acknowledged. "I'm not by any means saying I'm perfect. But I feel very good about our culture here, because a lot of our top leaders have embraced it."

The Huffington Post is hardly the only web media company with a reputation as an arduous place to work. Nor is Huffington the only editor in chief considered capricious and exasperating by employees. But she is surely the first described in those terms to install hammocks in a newsroom. Only someone with her unique combination of drive and outward placidity could run a tremendously popular, hugely productive website and then begin a second career chastening us for our addiction to the Internet. Somehow she has pulled it off. In her site's parenting section, some of the most successful posts target moms who are checking their Facebook feeds late at night, apparently yearning to be told that they shouldn't be on Facebook at that hour. "You know, posts about, 'Stop procrastinating and go sleep,' 'Disconnect your devices,' " said Ethan Fedida, the site's senior social media editor. "They go crazy for it."

It's as though Huffington is spreading an illness while simultaneously peddling the cure. Call it hypocrisy, but it testifies to her savvy. The business of web media is figuring out what people want — and if what we want is contradictory, why shouldn't Huffington profit from that contradiction?

Huffington may be engaged in a bit of wishful projection when she presents herself as an apostle of serenity. But it is a veneer she never drops, at least in public. At the Barnes & Noble event for "Thrive" last year, the one moderated by Katie Couric, a young woman rose during the question-and-answer session.

"What do you say to employers who are now seeking people specifically to work in social media?" she asked. "Our job is to be connected 24-7, where we have to manage your Facebook, your Instagram, your

Twitter, your Pinterest. How do we detox when we're told we have to be in the social-media revolution in order to earn our living?"

After thinking for a moment, Huffington suggested that she tell her employer that tweets can be scheduled in advance, so she doesn't have to be awake at all hours. Remind your boss that people are paid for their judgment, Huffington added, not their endurance. Couric then asked the young woman, "You think your boss would be receptive to that?"

"No," she said, flatly.

All eyes turned back to Huffington. Some bosses are toxic, she offered, so start looking for a new job. With a smile, she added: "We're hiring."

DAVID SEGAL is a business reporter for The Times.

F.T.C. Guidelines on Native Ads Aim to Prevent Deception

BY SYDNEY EMBER | DEC. 22, 2015

A LIST FOR PASTA LOVERS. An article about sleep deprivation. A web page detailing the history of cocaine traffickers.

Advertisers and publishers say these types of ads — known as native ads and packaged to look like journalism — are less intrusive and more appealing (not to mention more likely to be shared on social media) than other online ads. But consumer advocates say this native advertising can be intentionally misleading, and they have long called for some kind of federal regulation.

On Tuesday, the Federal Trade Commission issued a guide on native advertising intended to prevent customers from being deceived. The long-awaited guidelines function as a warning shot to the online ad industry and lay out for the first time how advertisers and publishers should deploy and label native ads.

The agency states, for instance, that advertisers "should not use terms such as 'Promoted' or 'Promoted Stories,' which in this context are at best ambiguous and potentially could mislead consumers that advertising content is endorsed by a publisher site." The F.T.C. also provides guidance on where disclosures should appear. If a native ad appears as a user scrolls down a web page, for example, a disclosure should not appear below the ad.

"People browsing the web, using social media, or watching videos have a right to know if they're seeing editorial content or an ad," Jessica L. Rich, director of the F.T.C.'s Bureau of Consumer Protection, said in a statement.

The F.T.C.'s guidance caps a long period of growth in native advertising, which mimics the look and feel of the host site.

But proponents of the ads contend that any rules could stymie the development of a tool that has become an increasingly important source of revenue for publishers. The practice has grown ever more popular in recent years as advertisers and publishers — including Forbes, Yahoo, BuzzFeed and The New York Times — have sought to reach savvy web users who increasingly block or simply ignore traditional online ads. And native ads have only grown more popular as consumers spend more time on their mobile phones, whose small screens have prompted marketers to look beyond intrusive banner ads and pop-ups. The Association of National Advertisers reported in January that nearly two-thirds of marketers surveyed said they planned to increase their spending on native advertising this year.

"Native is so organic," said Henry Tajer, the global chief executive of IPG Mediabrands. "It's like ivy."

The tactic now called native advertising is not new — many radio ads, magazine inserts and infomercials, for example, have long used a similar strategy. But native ads have grown more sophisticated online, and the line between marketing and journalism has blurred.

In their more basic forms, sponsored stories and blog posts, sometimes created by the publishers themselves, appear alongside news articles and other content. (Forbes's BrandVoice, for instance, allows advertisers like Fidelity and IBM to produce their own editorial content, which then appears on the Forbes site in the same style as an article done by the magazine.)

Other types of native ads include posts on Facebook and Twitter, paid-search results, and recommended links.

But the way publishers designate native ads is inconsistent and often vague — a shaded box or a small label with some version of the phrase "sponsored by." What all native ads have in common is that their appearance blends in with the rest of the page; on first glance, it is often unclear that native ads are ads at all.

"Native advertising is product placement on digital steroids," said Jeffrey Chester, executive director of the Center for Digital Democracy. "There's no way that saying, 'This is an ad,' means anything."

The rise of automated ad buying and the ability to show tailored ads to specific groups of people means advertisers can now serve native ads to targeted consumers based on their online behavior. A user who recently searched for doctors in Los Angeles might see a sponsored article for trusted physicians in California.

These kinds of targeted native ads have drawn particular concern from consumer-privacy advocates, who say no amount of labeling can make them less nefarious.

Mr. Chester, who sent several memos and letters to the F.T.C. about native ads, expressed concern that the F.T.C.'s guidance did not address how advertisers are using data to serve consumers specific native ads based on their interests and online behavior.

"What's needed is a 21st-century set of safeguards that enable consumers to control the data used to deliver them ads, especially formats like native that are specially designed to be disguised as content," Mr. Chester said in a statement.

Some industry executives warned that the guidelines could be seen as toothless: The F.T.C. is an enforcement agency and its recommendations are not laws. Still, publishers and advertisers who do not comply with the guidelines risk being held out as examples of bad actors. There could also be financial sanctions.

Marketers and publishers, however, worry that the guidelines could stifle further advancements in an area that they both have come to increasingly rely on.

"As soon as you start to standardize things and put guidelines around things, you limit the level of creativity and innovation that is able to occur," said Mark Howard, the chief revenue officer of Forbes Media. "If you put out stringent guidelines, are you going to put people back in the box?"

How Sponsored Content Is Becoming King in a Facebook World

BY JOHN HERRMAN | JULY 24, 2016

FOR SOME PUBLISHERS unsettled by a fast-changing online advertising business, sponsored content has provided much-needed relief.

In recent years, publications large and small have invested in teams to make sponsored content — written stories, videos or podcasts that look and feel like journalistic content — hoping to make up for declines in conventional advertising. To varying degrees, they have succeeded.

Younger companies like Vice and BuzzFeed have built whole businesses around the concept. The Atlantic expects three-quarters of its digital ad revenue to come from sponsored content this year. Slate, the web publisher, says that about half of its ad revenue comes from native ads, as sponsored content is also called, and the other half from traditional banner or display ads. Many major newspapers, including The New York Times, have declared sponsored content to be an important part of their strategies.

But as the relationship between publishers and social platforms like Facebook grows closer — and as more straightforward forms of advertising are devalued by ad-blocking and industry automation, the role, and definition, of sponsored content has shifted. Now, publishers, social media companies and advertisers are negotiating new relationships.

Audiences have migrated away from news websites and toward Facebook and other social media destinations, which for a competitive price can provide advertisers access to larger and more finely targeted groups of people, challenging the value of a publisher's own channels. With a weaker claim over audiences, publishers have been left to compete for advertising on different terms, leaning less on the size or demographics of their readerships, and more on the sorts of campaigns they can engineer for advertisers — campaigns that are then used across the internet.

"The differences between five years ago and now, in client expectations, are enormous," said Keith Hernandez, the president of Slate.

The resulting arrangements are more client-agency than advertiser-publisher, and advertisers are looking to media companies for a full range of services, from the production of campaigns to the often paid-for placement of the content across the internet and social media.

"We have the basic building blocks of a full-service agency," said Jon Slade, the chief commercial officer of The Financial Times. And The New York Times recently characterized the work of its T Brand Studio as "platform-agnostic."

As it has for traditional editorial content, Facebook has become a primary distributor for many publications' sponsored posts, even though outside sponsored content was not officially permitted until April, when the social network published formal guidelines.

Facebook's welcome of sponsored posts was broadly seen as a promising and necessary development. But some publishers were troubled by the manner in which Facebook said it would display sponsored posts and by how much power it put in the hands of advertisers.

Under Facebook's system, all advertisers must be disclosed and displayed as co-authors under the post or video, a level of disclosure that is required by the Federal Trade Commission.

In addition, these advertisers are now privy to a wide range of information about their sponsored content posted on Facebook — something that once was visible only to the publisher. They also get a deeper and more profound layer of data: They can see how much money was spent on Facebook promotion to drive traffic to the post in order to meet targets, a common and sometimes lucrative practice for publishers, who have been able to significantly mark up the price on such distribution.

What's more, Facebook invites the advertiser to pay to promote their sponsored content on their own, making them less reliant on the publisher for distribution.

From Facebook's point of view, this transparency eliminates inefficiency — why let middlemen charge extra for an audience that Facebook is selling? But for publishers who sold advertisers on their ability not just to create posts but to make sure they are seen, either through clever promotion or paid placement, such visibility can be deflating.

This change poses a persistent and tantalizing question to increasingly savvy advertisers: Could we just attract eyes to our posts ourselves? And if not now, maybe soon?

The change also discourages any illusions about how easy it could be for publishers to make money from native advertising. Sponsored content — which, in 2016, often means video — is expensive to produce and difficult to do well. Controlling distribution, albeit through Facebook, was for some a more profitable lever, and a way to pad deals that, while often growing in size, offered thin margins.

This is, of course, a boon to advertisers. "Many native campaigns are quite expensive, and if you limit the work you're doing to the creation of content, and leave the distribution to the brand, then it can become more affordable," said Stephanie Losee, head of content for Visa.

With less ability to charge for distribution, on their own channels or others, and a growing dependence on margin-squeezing outside platforms, publishers may be left to compete with creative agencies on their turf. Publishers becoming ad agencies, in other words, means competing not just with one another, but with the agencies that already exist.

In this nascent new order, competitors are defined largely by their limitations. While the terms and prices that publishers can accept from advertisers are set by the need to support a connected news or entertainment organization — the reason they chose this controversial path in the first place — conventional agencies are hampered by a dependence on lucrative TV work, from which they are accustomed to low volumes and high margins. Accordingly, publishers' pitches often focus on price: their ability to create more content for less.

Such a situation, in which publishers join a broader competition for advertising production dollars, would be a testament to how much and how quickly media distribution has changed. Publishers may get back in the running for advertising deals lost in recent years, but much like the editorial content they produce, their ads will succeed or fail in contexts over which they have less and less control.

Bryan Goldberg, founder of the women's website Bustle, views these changes with optimism, at least as far as they affect larger publishers. "Gross margins have slightly decreased, but not anywhere near enough to offset the upward movement in scale," he said.

For smaller publishers, or those without backing from venture capital, the situation is less heartening. "Running a full-scale sales, marketing and operations team requires tens of millions of dollars of annual expenses," Mr. Goldberg said.

Facebook, for its part, has provided a preview of how such a system might mature. A program that the company calls Anthology is meant to help video publishers "lend brands their creativity, storytelling expertise and video production know-how." It is being used by companies like Vox Media and Vice with advertising clients to produce videos that will then be promoted on Facebook.

Started last year, and quietly expanding to include more publishers, Anthology offers hints at what a platform marketplace managed from the top down might look like. It is tightly controlled, with a clear division of labor: The advertiser pays; the publisher creates; Facebook promotes. (Snapchat recently introduced a similar program, matching clients with a mix of publishers and ad agencies for campaigns.)

For now, despite uncertainty, publishers will most likely keep pushing forward. "It's kind of past the point of turning back. You kind of have to see if it can work," said Joe Lazauskas, editor of Contently, a content marketing and editorial firm. "There's not a lot of alternatives."

Ms. Losee, who previously ran the sponsored content operation for Politico, the politics news website, suggested that publishers' half-decade push into online native advertising will ultimately help them, but only up to a point.

"Sponsored content can't replace the revenue from traditional advertising," she said. "I think the future business model for publishers, in this disintermediation of the media era, is a work in progress."

Shocker! Facebook Changes Its Algorithm to Avoid 'Clickbait'

BY MIKE ISAAC AND SYDNEY EMBER | AUG. 4, 2016

FACEBOOK SAYS IT PLANS to marginalize what it considers to be "clickbait" news stories from publishers in its news feed, in another step to keep its 1.71 billion members regularly coming back to its social network.

In a change to its news feed algorithm on Thursday, Facebook said certain types of headlines would be classified as clickbait, those that "withhold or distort information." Those stories will then appear less frequently in users' feeds, the company said.

"We want publishers to post content that people care about, and we think people care about headlines that are much more straightforward," Adam Mosseri, Facebook's vice president for product management for the news feed, said in an interview.

Facebook has been working to maintain the integrity of the news feed to keep users happy and spending as much time on Facebook as possible. The Silicon Valley company constantly tweaks its algorithms, and in June it made a sweeping set of changes that would rank publisher content in general less favorably in the news feed.

Thursday's algorithm change is not the first time Facebook has cracked down on clickbait. In 2014, the company said it was moving to feature spamlike articles less prominently by looking at other factors, such as if a user has "liked" and then quickly "unliked" a story that appeared in the feed. Other factors, such as how much time people spent reading an article after clicking on it, also contributed to Facebook's clickbait calculations.

Thursday's announcement goes a step further. Facebook spent months classifying phrases commonly used in clickbait headlines. Mr. Mosseri offered examples like "The Dog Barked at the Deliveryman and His Reaction Was Priceless," or "When She Looked Under Her Couch Cushions and Saw THIS ... I Was SHOCKED!"

The company's algorithms then took note of the websites from which the articles were coming, and could detect patterns of traffic coming from those sites over time. That process was then automated, and content identified as clickbait will now appear lower in the news feed than before. Mr. Mosseri likened the practice to a kind of email spam filtering process.

The move will most likely heighten the anxiety of publishers that rely heavily on Facebook for traffic and often complain about having little insight into the company's decision-making on how its all-powerful algorithm functions.

The social network's vast user base and sophisticated targeting capabilities allow publishers to reach new audiences far beyond the direct traffic a media company receives at its own site. As a result, Facebook has been able to largely dictate the terms on which it engages with publishers, which have few other options for distributing their articles.

Julie Hansen, the president and chief operating officer of the online publication Business Insider, said it would take Facebook's latest algorithm change under consideration.

"We don't do what we consider to be clickbaity headlines," she said, "but we'll certainly consider Facebook's guidance when we look to post our content onto Facebook and adapt the headlines if needed."

Facebook said that publishers that have clickbaitlike headlines and are ranked lower because of the algorithm change will have the opportunity to change their ways and rise again in the rankings.

Some publishers are now betting on a future beyond total reliance on Facebook, as companies like Snapchat and Google offer media companies other avenues to distribute their work.

"Today we're at peak Facebook — Facebook dominates everything," said Zachary Kaplan, a vice president at the investment firm General Atlantic, which has invested in digital media companies like BuzzFeed and Vox Media.

"We will naturally evolve to a place where there will be more competition among digital distributors," he said, "and that would result in, naturally, more leverage for publishers."

For now, Facebook said it planned to improve relationships with publishers by becoming more transparent about its news feed practices. Mr. Mosseri regularly meets with publishers to discuss algorithm changes.

"It's becoming clear to us how there's a lot of anxiety over what we do," Mr. Mosseri said. "I spend a lot of time trying to ease that anxiety."

Good at Skipping Ads? No, You're Not

REVIEW | BY TIM WU | NOV. 25, 2016

BLACK OPS ADVERTISING
Native Ads, Content Marketing, and the Covert World of the Digital Sell
By Mara Einstein
248 pp. OR Books. Paper, $18.

I DON'T OFTEN watch late night television, which may be why I was caught unawares. Jimmy Fallon's opening monologue began hilariously enough, when abruptly he pivoted to a series of inexplicably weak jokes centered on a forthcoming football game. It slowly dawned on me that I was watching a commercial for NBC's "Sunday Night Football," albeit one baked right into the opening monologue and delivered by Fallon himself.

The realization that something you thought to be "real" is actually an advertisement is an increasingly common, if unsettling, sensation. Mara Einstein calls it "content confusion," and if her book, "Black Ops Advertising," is right, we're in for even more such trickery, indeed a possible future where nearly everything becomes hidden commercial propaganda of one form or another. She forecasts the potential of a "world where there is no real content: Everything we experience is some form of sales pitch."

Einstein, a former advertising executive turned media professor (who, among other things, worked campaigns for Uncle Ben's and Miller Lite), makes it clear that things were not always this way. Once upon a time the line between editorial and advertising, if not exactly a Chinese wall, was somewhat clearer. Einstein's well-researched and accomplished book is mainly about the effort to tear down that wall. The sledgehammers and pick axes in this case are things like "sponsored content," "native advertising" and "content marketing" designed to fool you into thinking they are real. Such stealth advertising may entertain or inform, yet it also brands, or more cleverly,

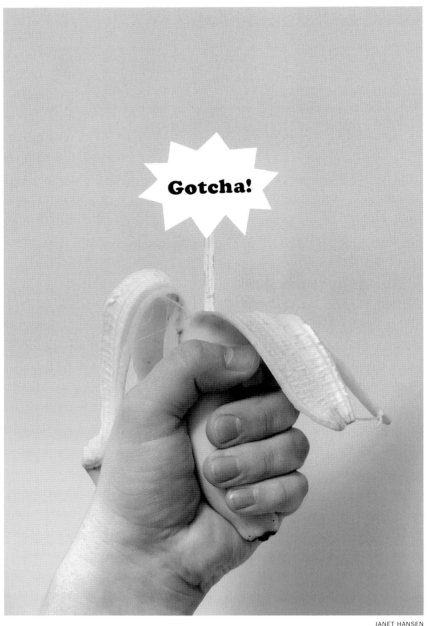

JANET HANSEN

facilitates a later branding exercise or sales pitch. The handoff can be smooth enough that you don't notice you've been steered to exit through the gift shop.

"Black Ops" presents some startling examples of stealth advertising. Remember that guy who in 2012 jumped out of a helium balloon at 128,000 feet for a new world record? Covered widely in the media, it was all, according to Einstein, a disguised Red Bull marketing campaign, but one where Red Bull's role was so discreet as to be almost invisible. You may also recall the audacious "tagging" of Air Force One by a graffiti artist named Marc Ecko, which has been viewed nearly a million times on YouTube. It was a hoax intended for the branding of a clothing and accessories label. That "ad" fooled so many members of the public and press that it was awarded the top prize for digital media at the annual Cannes Lions advertising festival.

The book is slightly guilty of exaggerating the novelty of present-day advertising techniques. Content that doubles as brand advertising is not exactly new. In the 1980s, "The Transformers" and "G.I. Joe" were popular children's cartoons but also advertisements, and so of course was the much beloved "Mickey Mouse Club" back in the 1960s. The idea of inventing media stories for commercial purpose also has a long pedigree, dating to at least the late 1920s, when Lucky Strike staged a protest (the "torches of liberty") featuring attractive women demanding the right to smoke outdoors as a part of suffragist liberation (yielding, ultimately, an equal right to lung cancer). Subliminal advertising, perhaps the blackest of all black ops, was popular in the 1950s, until it was banned. The difference, Einstein argues, lies in how much effort is going toward the dark arts. It is, she suggests, for one simple reason: that we, the public, are so good at avoiding or ignoring traditional advertising. We are fickle fish, cynical creatures who have already been hooked so many times that the simpler lures no longer work.

We avoid ads using devices as simple as the remote control (originally conceived as an ad-avoidance technology) and as sophisticated as ad-blocking phones (thanks, Apple). Many of us have developed a mental blindness that helps us see through advertising as if it were not there. Indeed, ad avoidance has become a lifestyle, so much so that some people will simply declare, "I don't watch advertising" the same way one might declare adherence to a gluten-free diet.

Einstein's book wanders from its main topic into a fuller review of contemporary advertising practice, including pseudo-engagement on social media, mass harvesting of private data and other unappealing practices. Perhaps the most important contribution she makes is providing a clear sense of what free content actually costs. There was a time when the idealists among us prophesied that the 21st century would be a golden age of free stuff, powered by a culture of sharing, and that targeted advertising would be a blessing for consumers. Today that vision has soured and even seems like a bad joke given how plagued we are by the rise of stealth advertising, the invasions of privacy, the proliferation of clickbait and stalking advertising, and the general degradation of much of the web.

Einstein is not enthusiastic about contemporary advertising practice, and few of us are likely to regard constant deception as attractive. But what's the remedy? One, briefly mentioned by Einstein, is legal. The Federal Trade Commission regards advertising posing as legitimate content to be an illegal form of "consumer deception." Einstein calls for more enforcement, but admits that it's not easy. What does one do, for example, about the many movies (like "The Transformers") and reality shows ("Keeping Up With the Kardashians") that are simultaneously entertainment and advertisement?

Einstein is not the first former marketing executive to turn on her profession; James Rorty, in 1934, wrote of his colleagues: "They are dead men. Their bones are Bakelite. Their blood is water, their flesh is pallid — yes, prick them and they do not bleed." But unlike Rorty, who wanted to destroy advertising, she would prefer to save it: She is nostalgic for the recent past, when audiences sitting through commercials made deception unnecessary. But if that's the remedy, it is a lost cause: No one who figures out how to avoid advertising willingly goes back.

Einstein too quickly discards the most important remedy for advertising's abuses: paying for content. A broader historical view can remind us that ad-supported media competes with paid media (like HBO, film, books). Those who don't want to live in a world constantly trying to trick us into watching ads may have the most impact by voting with their dollars and starving the beast of the attention it needs to survive. Paying for things (Facebook, if it let you pay, Einstein tells us, might be $12 a year) strikes at the heart of the business model, and indeed a partial revolt is already underway, as suggested by the popularity of advertising-free subscription services like Netflix.

It is a reminder that advertising-supported entertainment is hardly indelible or eternal, but a relatively recent invention whose future is insecure. From this perspective, the rise of black ops advertising may be less a sign of power than of desperation.

TIM WU is the author of "The Attention Merchants: The Epic Struggle to Get Inside Our Heads."

CHAPTER 3

The Web Gets Personal, for Better and for Worse

As the personalized web took shape, users increasingly began to rely on invisible algorithms to tailor their experience to their tastes. These algorithms sort through a great deal of user data, not always willingly given by users. Many businesses thrived by the new, targeted markets this data provided. Some raised alarm, as Eli Pariser criticized the "filter bubbles" that limit our media diet to what we already know and like. Others were especially concerned by algorithms that appeared to target them by race.

When the Internet Thinks It Knows You

OPINION | BY ELI PARISER | MAY 22, 2011

ONCE UPON A TIME, the story goes, we lived in a broadcast society. In that dusty pre-Internet age, the tools for sharing information weren't widely available. If you wanted to share your thoughts with the masses, you had to own a printing press or a chunk of the airwaves, or have access to someone who did. Controlling the flow of information was an elite class of editors, producers and media moguls who decided what people would see and hear about the world. They were the Gatekeepers.

Then came the Internet, which made it possible to communicate with millions of people at little or no cost. Suddenly anyone with an

Internet connection could share ideas with the whole world. A new era of democratized news media dawned.

You may have heard that story before — maybe from the conservative blogger Glenn Reynolds (blogging is "technology undermining the gatekeepers") or the progressive blogger Markos Moulitsas (his book is called "Crashing the Gate"). It's a beautiful story about the revolutionary power of the medium, and as an early practitioner of online politics, I told it to describe what we did at MoveOn.org. But I'm increasingly convinced that we've got the ending wrong — perhaps dangerously wrong. There is a new group of gatekeepers in town, and this time, they're not people, they're code.

Today's Internet giants — Google, Facebook, Yahoo and Microsoft — see the remarkable rise of available information as an opportunity. If they can provide services that sift though the data and supply us with the most personally relevant and appealing results, they'll get the most users and the most ad views. As a result, they're racing to offer personalized filters that show us the Internet that they think we want to see. These filters, in effect, control and limit the information that reaches our screens.

By now, we're familiar with ads that follow us around online based on our recent clicks on commercial Web sites. But increasingly, and nearly invisibly, our searches for information are being personalized too. Two people who each search on Google for "Egypt" may get significantly different results, based on their past clicks. Both Yahoo News and Google News make adjustments to their home pages for each individual visitor. And just last month, this technology began making inroads on the Web sites of newspapers like The Washington Post and The New York Times.

All of this is fairly harmless when information about consumer products is filtered into and out of your personal universe. But when personalization affects not just what you buy but how you think, different issues arise. Democracy depends on the citizen's ability to engage with multiple viewpoints; the Internet limits such engagement when it offers up only information that reflects your already established point of view. While it's sometimes convenient to see only what you want to see, it's critical at other times that you see things that you don't.

Like the old gatekeepers, the engineers who write the new gatekeeping code have enormous power to determine what we know about the world. But unlike the best of the old gatekeepers, they don't see themselves as keepers of the public trust. There is no algorithmic equivalent to journalistic ethics.

Mark Zuckerberg, Facebook's chief executive, once told colleagues that "a squirrel dying in your front yard may be more relevant to your interests right now than people dying in Africa." At Facebook, "relevance" is virtually the sole criterion that determines what users see. Focusing on the most personally relevant news — the squirrel — is a great business strategy. But it leaves us staring at our front yard instead of reading about suffering, genocide and revolution.

There's no going back to the old system of gatekeepers, nor should there be. But if algorithms are taking over the editing function and determining what we see, we need to make sure they weigh variables beyond a narrow "relevance." They need to show us Afghanistan and Libya as well as Apple and Kanye.

Companies that make use of these algorithms must take this curative responsibility far more seriously than they have to date. They need to give us control over what we see — making it clear when they are personalizing, and allowing us to shape and adjust our own filters. We citizens need to uphold our end, too — developing the "filter literacy" needed to use these tools well and demanding content that broadens our horizons even when it's uncomfortable.

It is in our collective interest to ensure that the Internet lives up to its potential as a revolutionary connective medium. This won't happen if we're all sealed off in our own personalized online worlds.

ELI PARISER, the president of the board of MoveOn.org, is the author of "The Filter Bubble: What the Internet Is Hiding From You."

The Trouble With the Echo Chamber Online

BY NATASHA SINGER | MAY 28, 2011

ON THE WEB, we often see what we like, and like what we see. Whether we know it or not, the Internet creates personalized e-comfort zones for each one of us.

Give a thumbs up to a movie on Netflix or a thumbs down to a song on Pandora, de-friend a bore on Facebook or search for just about anything on Google: all of these actions feed into algorithms that then try to predict what we want or don't want online.

And what's wrong with that?

Plenty, according to Eli Pariser, the author of "The Filter Bubble: What the Internet Is Hiding From You." Personalization on the Web, he says, is becoming so pervasive that we may not even know what we're missing: the views and voices that challenge our own thinking.

"People love the idea of having their feelings affirmed," Mr. Pariser told me earlier this month. "If you can provide that warm, comfortable sense without tipping your hand that your algorithm is pandering to people, then all the better."

Mr. Pariser, the board president of the progressive advocacy group MoveOn.org, recounted a recent experience he had on Facebook. He went out of his way to "friend" people with conservative politics. When he didn't click on their updates as often as those of his like-minded contacts, he says, the system dropped the outliers from his news feed.

Personalization, he argues, channels people into feedback loops, or "filter bubbles," of their own predilections.

Facebook did not respond to e-mails seeking comment.

In an ideal world, the Web would be a great equalizer, opening up the same unlimited vistas to everyone. Personalization is supposed to streamline discovery on an individual level.

It's certainly convenient.

If you type "bank" into Google, the search engine recognizes your general location, sending results like "Bank of America" to users in the United States or "Bank of Canada" to those north of the border. If you choose to share more data, by logging into Gmail and enabling a function called Web history, Google records the sites you visit and the links you click. Now if you search for "apple," it learns and remembers whether you are looking for an iPad or a Cox's Orange Pippin.

If you're a foodie, says Jake Hubert, a Google spokesman, "over time, you'll see more results for apple the fruit not for Apple the computer, and that's based on your Web history."

The same idea applies at Netflix. As customers stream movies, the recommendation system not only records whether those viewers generally enjoy comedies but also can fine-tune suggestions to slapstick or more cerebral humor, says John Ciancutti, the company's vice president for personalization technology.

But, in a effort to single out users for tailored recommendations or advertisements, personalization tends to sort people into categories that may limit their options. It is a system that cocoons users, diminishing the kind of exposure to opposing viewpoints necessary for a healthy democracy, says Jaron Lanier, a computer scientist and the author of "You Are Not a Gadget."

"People tend to get into this echo chamber where more and more of what they see conforms to the idea of who some software thinks they are — like a Nascar dad who likes samurai swords," Mr. Lanier says. "You start to become more and more like the image of you because that is what you are seeing."

Mr. Lanier, who is currently doing research at a Microsoft lab, emphasized that his comments were his own personal opinions.

If you want to test your own views on personalization, you could try a party trick Mr. Pariser demonstrated earlier this year during a talk at the TED conference: ask some friends to simultaneously search Google for a controversial term like gun control or abortion. Then compare results.

CHRISTOPHE VORLET

"It's totally creepy if you think about it," said Tze Chun, a film-maker who agreed to participate in a similar experiment at a recent dinner party we both attended in Brooklyn. Five of us used our phones to search for "Is Osama really dead?," a phrase Mr. Chun suggested.

Although our top 10 results included the same link — to Yahoo Canada answers — in first place, two of us also received a link to a post on jewishjournal.com, a newspaper site. Meanwhile, Mr. Chun and two other filmmakers had links to more conspiratorial sites like deadbodies.info.

For Mr. Chun, who visits a variety of true-crime Web sites as part of his screenplay research but tends to favor sites that sell vintage T-shirts in his private life, the personalization felt a little too, well, personal.

"You are used to looking at the Internet voyeuristically," he said. "It's weird to have the Internet looking back at you and saying, 'Yeah, I remember things about what you have done' and gearing the searches to those sites."

With television, people can limit their exposure to dissenting opinions simply by flipping the channel, to, say, Fox from MSNBC. And, of course, viewers are aware they're actively choosing shows. The concern with personalization algorithms is that many consumers don't understand, or may not even be aware of, the filtering methodology.

Personalized Web services, Mr. Pariser says, could do more to show users a wider-angle view of the world.

But some of the most popular sites say they have already built diversity into their personalization platforms.

"People value getting information from a wide variety of perspectives, so we have algorithms in place designed specifically to limit personalization and promote variety in the results page," said Mr. Hubert, the Google spokesman. He added that the company looked forward to "carefully reviewing Mr. Pariser's analysis of this important issue."

At Netflix, the system recommends a mix of titles, some with high confidence of viewer enjoyment and others about which it is less sure, Mr. Ciancutti says. Netflix's flat monthly rate for unlimited streaming, he adds, encourages people to select films, like documentaries, that they might not have chosen otherwise.

Individual users could also do their part.

Mr. Pariser suggests people sign up for a range of feeds on Twitter, where the posts are unfiltered. Mr. Lanier suggests Tea Party members swap laptops for a day with progressives and observe the different results that turn up on one another's search engines.

If we don't chip away at the insulation of consensus, they caution, the promise of the World Wide Web could give way to a netherworld of narcissism Net.

What You Didn't Post, Facebook May Still Know

BY SOMINI SENGUPTA | MARCH 25, 2013

SAN FRANCISCO — Debra Aho Williamson, an advertising industry analyst and devoted coffee drinker, was intrigued by a promotion that popped up on her Facebook page recently. Sign up for a Starbucks loyalty card, it said, and get $5 off.

"When I saw that, I thought, I'm already a member of their loyalty club," she said. "Why don't they know that?"

Despite the streams of data Facebook has collected about people like Ms. Williamson, the social network needs to know its users much better if it is going to become, as the company hopes, the Web's most effective advertising platform. And Facebook is scrambling to do just that.

In shaping its targeted advertising strategy, it is no longer relying solely on what Facebook users reveal about themselves. Instead, it is tapping into outside sources of data to learn even more about them — and to sell ads that are more finely targeted to them. Facebook says that this way, marketers will be able to reach the right audience for the right products, and consumers will see advertisements that are, as the company calls it, "relevant" to them.

In late February, Facebook announced partnerships with four companies that collect lucrative behavioral data, from store loyalty card transactions and customer e-mail lists to divorce and Web browsing records.

They include Acxiom, which aggregates data from a variety of sources, including financial services companies, court records and federal government documents; Datalogix, which claims to have a database on the spending habits of more than 100 million Americans in categories like fine jewelry, cough medicine and college tuition; and Epsilon, which also collects transaction data from retailers.

Acxiom and Datalogix are among nine companies that the Federal Trade Commission is investigating to see how they collect and use consumer data.

Facebook's fourth partner is BlueKai, based in Cupertino, Calif., which creates tracking cookies for brands to monitor customers who visit their Web sites. That data can be used to show an advertisement when those users log on to Facebook.

"Our goal is to improve the relevance of ads people see on Facebook and the efficacy of marketing campaigns," Gokul Rajaram, product director for ads at Facebook, said in an interview on Friday.

In announcing the partnerships, Facebook said it would allow, for instance, a carmaker to customize an advertisement to users interested in a new car.

The push to refine targeted advertising reflects the company's need to increase its revenue. Its shares are worth far less than its ambitious initial public offering price of $38 a share last May, and Wall Street wants to see it take concrete steps to prove to advertisers that it can show the right promotions to the right users and turn them into customers.

The partnerships are part of a continuum of efforts by Facebook to hone targeted advertising. Last fall, it invited potential advertisers to provide the e-mail addresses of their customers; Facebook then found those customers among its users and showed them ads on behalf of the brands.

JackThreads, a members-only online men's retailer, tried this tactic recently. Of the two million customer e-mails it had on file, Facebook found more than two-thirds of them on the social network, aided in part by the fact that JackThreads allows members to sign in using Facebook login credentials. Facebook then showed those customers ads for the items they had once eyed on the JackThreads site.

The nudge seemed to get people to open up their pocketbooks. Sales increased 26 percent at JackThreads, according to AdParlor, an agency that buys the company's advertisements on Facebook.

Targeted advertising bears important implications for consumers. It could mean seeing advertisements based not just on what they "like" on Facebook, but on what they eat for breakfast, whether they buy khakis or jeans and whether they are more likely to give their wives roses or tulips on their wedding anniversary. It means that even things people don't reveal on Facebook may be discovered from their online and offline proclivities.

Facebook says that in devising targeted ads, no identifying information about users is shared with advertisers. E-mail addresses and Facebook user names are encrypted and then matched. Users can opt out of seeing specific brand advertisements on their page, and they can opt out of receiving any targeted messages by visiting each third-party data partner's Web site.

That is a somewhat complicated process, though, which has prompted the Electronic Frontier Foundation to issue step-by-step instructions. The foundation suggests that consumers who want to avoid ubiquitous tracking install tools to block Web trackers and be mindful about sharing their e-mail addresses with marketers. Facebook declined to provide data on how often users opt out of seeing ads.

"It's ultimately good for the users," Mr. Rajaram said. "They get to see better, more relevant ads from brands and businesses they care about and that they have a prior relationship with."

He added, "There is no information on users that's being shared that they haven't shared already."

Whether Facebook users will enjoy seeing "relevant" ads or be alienated by more intensive tracking remains to be seen.

At the very least, said Ms. Williamson, an analyst with the research firm eMarketer, consumers will be "forced to become more aware of the data trail they leave behind them and how companies are putting all that data together in new ways to reach them." She knows, for instance, that if she uses her supermarket loyalty card to buy cornflakes, she can expect to see a cornflakes advertisement when she logs in to Facebook.

After all, she said, "data is the new currency of marketing."

These efforts speak volumes about the data trail that consumers leave every day, online and off — a trail that can follow them back to Facebook or to any other advertising platform on the Web. They offer lucrative information every time they provide their e-mail address to a dressmaker or a doctor, and even when they give their ZIP code at the checkout counter. They use loyalty cards to buy snorkeling gear or antidepressants. They browse a retail Web site, leaving a detailed portrait of whether they are interested in ergonomic work chairs or nursery furniture.

Facebook said it was too early to reveal details about how the data collected through its new partnerships would be put to use by marketers.

1-800-Flowers, the online florist, said it had been experimenting with targeted ads on Facebook. What the company was most looking forward to was a new advertising conceit, which Facebook calls Looka-like, that would allow 1-800-Flowers to show its ads to other Facebook users who are similar to the company's known customers.

Christopher G. McCann, president of 1-800-Flowers, said he had no idea how Facebook planned to identify "look-alikes," only that it had promised to find potential new customers through a proprietary algo-rithm that matches demographic traits.

Last year, Facebook also introduced a so-called retargeting cam-paign. A travel Web site could track what its customers were looking at — hotels in New York, for instance — and show those customers an ad once they logged on to Facebook. The tracking is done by a piece of code embedded in the travel company's site.

For marketers, more data could mean getting closer to the ulti-mate goal of advertising: sending the right message to the right con-sumer at the right time.

When Facebook announced its targeted ad offerings, Justin Bazan, an optometrist in Park Slope, Brooklyn, immediately saw an oppor-tunity for his business. He combed through his office records for the e-mail addresses of patients who were overdue for an annual exam. Facebook matched most of those e-mails to Facebook user names, and Dr. Bazan paid $50 to show those users an advertisement. "You're overdue," the ad read. "Click here to make an appointment."

Within a week, more than 50 people had clicked on his ad, he said.

Dr. Bazan dismissed concerns about federal confidentiality laws that protect health information. Facebook, he said, encrypts the e-mail addresses furnished by any advertiser, including doctors.

Google and Facebook Face Criticism for Ads Targeting Racist Sentiments

BY SAPNA MAHESHWARI AND ALEXANDRA STEVENSON | SEPT. 15, 2017

GOOGLE AND FACEBOOK, the world's biggest sellers of online advertising, faced sharp criticism on Friday for allowing advertisers to direct ads to users who searched for or expressed an interest in racist sentiments and hate speech.

In response to two separate news reports exposing the issues, both companies said they would change how their systems worked.

The criticism began on Thursday after a report from ProPublica, a nonprofit news site, revealed that Facebook enabled advertisers to seek out self-described "Jew haters" and other anti-Semitic topics. The company responded by saying that it would restrict how advertisers targeted their audiences on the social network.

On Friday, an article from BuzzFeed reported how Google allowed the sale of ads tied to racist and bigoted keywords, and automatically suggested more offensive terms as part of that process. By midday, Google said it would work harder to halt offensive ads.

The incidents added to a growing awareness of the complicated — and powerful — automated advertising systems that have turned Facebook and Google into two of the world's most valuable companies. The companies have learned how to maximize their ability to connect any size of advertiser to highly tailored groups of people who use their services every day, collecting billions of dollars in the process.

But the potential misuse of those tools has become a national concern in the past year, particularly after Facebook disclosed last week that fake accounts based in Russia had purchased more than $100,000 worth of ads on divisive issues in the lead-up to the presidential election.

"It's shocking because it's illustrating the degree of targeting that's possible," said Eli Pariser, the author of "The Filter Bubble: How the New Personalized Web Is Changing What We Read and How We Think."

"But I think the critical piece of context is this is happening when we know that a foreign country used targeted Facebook ads to influence opinion around an election."

He added: "Before all of this, you could see the rise of targeted advertising, you could see the rise of social politics, but the conjunction of the two in this way feels new."

Facebook's self-service ad-buying platform allowed advertisers to direct ads to the news feeds of about 2,300 people who said they were interested in anti-Semitic subjects, according to the article by ProPublica. Facebook's algorithms automatically generated the categories from users' profiles.

Reporters from ProPublica tested Facebook advertising categories to see whether they could buy ads aimed at people who expressed interest in topics like "Jew hater," "How to burn jews," and "History of 'why jews ruin the world.' " The reporters paid $30 to promote ProPublica posts to the people affiliated with the anti-Semitic categories to ensure they were real options, according to the investigation, which noted that Facebook had approved the posts within 15 minutes.

Facebook said in a statement that users had entered the terms under the "employer" or "education" fields on their profiles. Doing so violated the company's policies, the company said, and led to their appearance on the ad-buying tool.

The company said it would remove targeting by such self-reported fields "until we have the right processes in place to help prevent this issue." It added that "hate speech and discriminatory advertising have no place on our platform."

After the ProPublica report, BuzzFeed conducted a similar test on Google, where ads are purchased based on potential search terms. The site reported that upon entering terms like "why do Jews ruin everything" and "white people ruin," the automated system suggested long lists of offensive "keyword ideas" like "black people ruin neighborhoods" and "Jewish parasites." It then allowed the purchase of some of the terms for ads.

Mark Zuckerberg, Facebook's chief executive, in April. A report by ProPublica said the social network's self-service ad-buying system let advertisers seek out self-described "Jew haters."

Google said that it informed advertisers when their ads were offensive and rejected, and that not all suggested keywords were eligible for purchase.

"In this instance, ads didn't run against the vast majority of these keywords, but we didn't catch all these offensive suggestions," Sridhar Ramaswamy, Google's senior vice president of ads, said in a statement. "That's not good enough, and we're not making excuses. We've already turned off these suggestions, and any ads that made it through, and will work harder to stop this from happening again."

The Daily Beast noted on Friday that Twitter was also allowing people to target ads based on some racial slurs. But the greater scrutiny is on Facebook and Google, given their sheer size and dominance of the online advertising business, which brings each company tens of billions of dollars in revenue a year.

Last week, Facebook representatives briefed the Senate and House Intelligence Committees, which are investigating Russian intervention in the election, about ads on the site. The company told congressional investigators that it had identified more than $100,000 worth of ads on hot-button issues that were traced back to a Russian company with links to the Kremlin.

The ads — about 3,000 of them — focused on divisive topics like gay rights, gun control, race and immigration, and they were linked to 470 fake accounts and pages that Facebook subsequently took down, according to its chief security officer. Facebook has not released copies of the ads to the public.

Last fall, Facebook came under fire after ProPublica reported that advertisers could use its targeting to exclude certain races, or what the social network called "ethnic affinities," from housing and employment ads, a potential violation of the Fair Housing Act of 1968 and the Civil Rights Act of 1964. Facebook, which assigns the updated term "multicultural affinity" to certain users based on their interests and activities on the site, no longer allows it to be used in ads for housing, employment or credit.

These series of problems with advertising make the company look unprepared to handle the power of its ad system, said Benjamin Edelman, an associate professor at Harvard Business School.

"They've created a very complicated ad platform — it has all kinds of options and doodads and things working automatically and manually, and they don't know what they built," Professor Edelman said. "The machine has a mind of its own."

Mr. Pariser said the types of targeting reported this week made a strong argument for increased disclosure of the funding behind political ads online, especially on Facebook. The Federal Election Commission voted on Thursday to seek public comment on disclosure requirements around online political ads, which advocates hope will lead to rules requiring more disclaimers revealing who paid for online content.

"This is drawing a new level of public awareness to how targeted advertising can be used to manipulate and affect politics and political conversation in ways that didn't used to be feasible at all or easy," Mr. Pariser said.

How Facebook's Oracular Algorithm Determines the Fates of Start-Ups

BY BURT HELM | NOV. 2, 2017

The platform is so good at "microtargeting" that many small e-commerce companies barely even bother advertising anywhere else.

NO ONE WOULD MISTAKE Ben Cogan and Jesse Horwitz for "brogrammers," the jockish male coders swaggering across the tech landscape. Nor are they hustlers, the relentlessly outgoing types who quit their jobs to gamble on audacious ventures. They are two bookish friends, ages 27 and 29, who until recently lived across the street from each other on the Upper West Side of Manhattan. Horwitz worked for Columbia University's endowment fund; Cogan had a job analyzing consumer behavior. Their hobbies are quiet. Cogan dreams of earning a Ph.D. in philosophy someday — "after all this is said and done," he says. Horwitz enjoys tracking various aspects of his life in Excel spreadsheets: restaurants visited, books read, jogs taken. Scrolling through those files, he says, fills him with a sort of data-based nostalgia. For years, the two men met for dinner every week or so, where talk often turned to business ideas. Spitballing plans for start-ups became their equivalent of fantasy football.

One night in the summer of 2015, over Sichuan at Han Dynasty on 85th Street, Cogan asked Horwitz for advice about his latest notion: selling contact lenses online. The contacts business was dominated by a handful of companies like Johnson & Johnson and Bausch & Lomb, which seemed to charge whatever they wanted — at least in Cogan's view, based on the price increases for his own lenses. Surely a low-cost competitor could tempt away customers. Cogan pulled his laptop from his bag and opened it at the table in the middle of dinner, pushing aside plates of dumplings and scallion pancakes. He had two plans to show Horwitz. They could sell a cheap disposable lens to doctors. Or they could mimic Cogan's employer, a wildly successful start-up called Harry's.

By late 2015, Harry's, which sold safety razors and shaving cream, was in the vanguard of upstart online retailers known as direct-to-consumer companies. The business model works like this: Firms sell only their own products, only through their own websites. By cutting out retailers and distributors, they can charge less for their specialty products than entrenched competitors. That year, Casper, then a direct-to-consumer mattress and bedding seller, was reported to be on track to exceed $100 million in sales in its second year of business. Dollar Shave Club, another seller of razors, had reached $152 million in revenue. Warby Parker, the eyeglasses purveyor that many credit with pioneering this business model in 2010, had recently closed an investment round that reportedly valued the company at $1.2 billion. Venture capitalists — convinced that consumers would increasingly patronize specialty online retailers as they grew more comfortable shopping online — were pouring money into direct-to-consumer start-ups, more than $2 billion over the past four years, according to CB Insights.

Horwitz, by now bored in his job, pushed Cogan to keep pursuing his idea and volunteered to help him do research. "It's hard to intellectualize whether an idea is good or not," Horwitz says. "You have to just start doing it and see."

By February 2016, after many nights and weekends of emailing Asian manufacturers and reading up on Food and Drug Administration compliance, the vision of a viable business was coming into focus. The pair had found an F.D.A.-approved manufacturer in Asia and figured out how to meet the necessary regulations. Still, Cogan was reluctant. He had been accepted to Wharton and had even put down a deposit. He believed that was the smarter option. At best, the contact-lens business would become a side project.

Before shelving their venture, they decided to try one more tack. They recruited two friends: Paul Rodgers, a buddy of Horwitz's from Columbia who knew how to write computer code, and Dan Rosen, a friend of Cogan's from Bronx Science who was handy with Adobe Photoshop and Illustrator. Together the four built what is known in the world of online retailing as a demand experiment. The technique, credited to Harry's founders (who give away its basic code), amounts to a two-page website. The first page explained the concept of a monthly subscription for contacts and asked those who were interested to submit their email addresses. Visitors who did so were taken to a second page and were made an offer: Share this referral code with friends, and if enough of them sign up, you'll get free contacts.

They posted a link to their site on the walls of about 40 Facebook friends. Within a few days, not only had their own friends signed up, but friends of friends of friends had, too — some 2,000 people in all. Some of those distant connections were even evangelizing the company on their own Facebook walls. "It went mini-viral," Cogan says.

He and Horwitz applied to tech incubators — organizations that invest in and coach young companies in exchange for minority stakes — using the demand experiment as one slide in their 16-page PowerPoint presentation. They pitched a few venture capitalists based in New York as well. They decided that if they were admitted to an incubator, they would work on the project full time. If not, Cogan would go to Wharton. By April, they had not only been called back for interviews with five incubators; venture funds were also offering to invest a total of $3.5 million in their idea.

Cogan dropped his Wharton plans. He and Horwitz ordered 50,000 contact lenses and, with Rosen as creative director and Rodgers as chief technology officer, began working out of their investors' offices, stacking boxes and boxes of lenses along the walls by their desks. They eventually named their enterprise Hubble, after the orbiting telescope that can see into deep space.

Facebook helped them succeed with their demand test; now it would generate their first sales. During the summer of 2016, a friend of one of Hubble's prospective investors, a start-up veteran named Joshua Liberson, recommended that the founders try a new type of Facebook advertising called Lead Ads. No outside website was needed: Would-be customers simply clicked a button on the ad to submit their email addresses, directly from Facebook. Hubble directed its ads to ZIP codes in New York and Chicago, where they had already signed up optometrists willing to write prescriptions. After people clicked the ads, Horwitz emailed them to coordinate appointments and take their orders.

When Hubble's online store opened officially on Nov. 1, 2016, Cogan and Horwitz knew how to run a Facebook advertising campaign, and they were confident it would continue to generate sales. They planned to spend the additional $3.7 million they raised almost entirely on Facebook ads.

In 2017, everyone seems to be wondering: Is Facebook taking over the world? Most of us now realize that the social network has become far more than a repository for selfies and political rants of its more than two billion users. To ad sellers, Facebook is now a gluttonous monster, which, along with Google, is gobbling up the digital advertising business in the United States; according to Pivotal Research Group, the two companies controlled 70 percent of the market and most of the growth in 2016. From the perspective of American intelligence agencies, Facebook is practically a weapon, used by a company linked to the Kremlin to foment extremism and influence the 2016 presidential election with at least $100,000 worth of targeted ads. For those with privacy concerns, Facebook plays the role of Big Brother, compiling ever more data on what we like, what we post and what we buy and even tracking where we are both online and in the physical world by tapping into the GPS locator on our phones.

In considering Facebook's far-reaching influence, it's worth keeping in mind the perspective of the more than five million advertisers whose money is financing the social network's rampant growth. For them, Facebook and Instagram, which the company also owns, are the stuff of fantasy — grand bazaars on a scale never seen before. By advertising directly in users' news feeds, companies can, at any time of day, target potential customers at moments when they are often bored and open to novelty. What better time to hear a product pitch?

"Facebook created the world's greatest infomercial," says Roger

McNamee, a founder of Elevation Partners, who invested early in Facebook but has since become critical of the company's influence. "It's really inexpensive to produce ads and unbelievably inexpensive to reach exactly the market that you're looking for." As a result, Facebook has become especially lucrative for companies trying to sell new products online. The leaders of more than half a dozen new online retailers all told me they spent the greatest portion of their ad money on Facebook and Instagram.

"In the start-up-industrial complex, it's like a systematic transfer of money" from venture-capital firms to start-ups to Facebook, says Charlie Mulligan, the founder of BrewPublik, which uses a "Beergorithm" to deliver personalized selections of craft beers to customers every month. At 500 Startups, the tech incubator based in Silicon Valley that funded BrewPublik, Facebook advertising is a topic covered in classes. In fact, social-network advertising is an assumed prerequisite for anyone studying marketing at a tech incubator these days — or at any business school across the country. "There is a formula for this stuff," Mulligan says. "And the reason why there is a formula is because it works."

The process is easy, cheap and effective. With a few hundred dollars and a morning's effort, an entrepreneur can place his or her ads before social-media users that same afternoon. Companies unsure which ads are best can upload a handful of them and let Facebook's artificial-intelligence software test their efficacy. If they don't know who should see their ads, they can embed code on their websites that enables Facebook to monitor the traffic and then show ads to recent visitors. Or companies can send the email addresses of their existing customers to Facebook, and it will locate their Facebook accounts and put ads in front of so-called Lookalikes, users who like and click on the same things that your proven fan base does. It's all about as straightforward as setting up an online dating profile. Steph Korey, a founder of Away, a luggage company based in New York that opened in 2015, says that when the company was starting, it made $5 for every $1 it spent on Facebook Lookalike ads.

The ease of opening a business on Facebook has in turn spawned a wild proliferation of specialty digital sellers that depend on the social network's algorithm to find their early customers. Many of them follow the same playbook and even share a similar aesthetic. They spend money on traditional public relations, on sponsored links that appear next to Google search results and on "influencer" marketing, or giving away their product to people with large social-media followings, in hopes of creating buzz. Then they buy ads on Facebook and Instagram. Inevitably you will encounter them there: They feature a sleek photograph or a video loop of a product — a wood-handled water filter, woolen shoes, an electric toothbrush. At the top, in bold, the company's name appears, often ringing with the same friendly, typically two-syllable whimsy. Soma. Allbirds. Goby.

"Sometimes we'll look at each other and say, 'God, there are just so many of them,' " says Ellie Wheeler, a partner at the venture fund Greycroft Partners, which invested in Hubble last year. Her firm has also taken ownership stakes in Thrive Market, which sells health foods; Plated, a meal-kit delivery service; Trunk Club, which mails a box of clothes to its customers; and Eloquii, a fast-fashion retailer specializing in plus sizes.

While not all of these companies and others like them will survive, plenty are encroaching on established brands, which are taking the threat seriously. In July 2016, Unilever, the European consumer-products conglomerate, acquired Dollar Shave Club for a reported $1 billion. In June, Walmart agreed to buy Bonobos, an internet-based apparel brand, for $310 million. Companies that sell products exclusively online continue to grow faster than any other type of retailer in the United States — some 17 percent annually since 2011, more than six times the rate of retail over all, according to Euromonitor International.

And Facebook has even been taking steps to influence offline sales, in order to bring traditional retailers into its orbit. In September, the social network introduced a tool that lets businesses with physical stores show ads to shoppers and their Lookalikes even if they visit the store but don't buy anything. Day by day, Facebook is extending its reach further and further into the American marketplace.

One afternoon in March, I watched as Rosen selected three new ads from an extensive photo shoot the week before, his third in four months. Rosen resembled a sleep-deprived new parent — mussed hair, dull gaze. He spoke in a monotone. He attributed his fatigue, I would learn later, to Facebook's artificial-intelligence software that placed Hubble's ads. Rosen and his colleagues simply referred to it as "the algorithm."

The basic building block of Facebook advertising is an ad set. It consists of the ads themselves and choices in three other categories: audience, goal and budget. That day, Rosen was designing a set to reach an audience of people on Instagram who had visited hubblecontacts.com in the past 30 days. His goal was "conversions," or persuading users who had seen the company's ad to make a purchase. Finally, he set a budget of $1,000 per day. He uploaded the three images. Now they were ready to be tested, to see if any of them were winners in the eyes of users and the algorithm.

What happened at 8 a.m. the next morning, when the ad set became active, was complex — and far removed from human sight. Just before Facebook places an advertisement in a user's feed, it holds a sort of instantaneous auction to determine which advertiser gets the space. The amount of each advertiser's bid is influenced by its budget size, of course, but the algorithm also weighs what it knows about the company, the ad and the individual Facebook user. Seeking to act like an intuitive matchmaker, the algorithm draws inferences from personal interests, current online behavior, the user's potential value to each advertiser and the ad's general appeal. Sometimes the winner is the advertiser that offered Facebook the most money. Sometimes the algorithm decides you are more likely to click a different ad and awards the space to that advertiser for less money.

This detailed handicapping process involves thousands of advertisers per auction. Millions of auctions take place every minute as users across Facebook load their feeds. The process is never the same twice. The algorithm is constantly learning, using past results to inform how it weighs bids in the next auction. The intent, Facebook says, is to maximize value for everybody: to pair the advertiser with its likeliest customers, and to show ads that users want to see. And, of course, to make money for Facebook.

But from Rosen's perspective, nothing much had happened before he ambled into the office a little after 10 a.m. Facebook had spent a grand total of $1.86 on his ads. It had shown the first ad to 51 people, the second to 45 and the third to only two. The first ad had been clicked once. Rosen, unperturbed, poured himself a cup of coffee from the single-serve machine. The algorithm takes a little while to get warmed up, he said. "In an hour, it'll get exciting."

Twenty minutes later, Rosen refreshed his browser. The Ads Manager window displayed the latest numbers: Rosen could see only the results, not the process that produced them, but it seemed as if the click had inspired the algorithm to favor the first ad. During those 20 minutes, the first ad appeared before 76 more people — that is, it won 76 more auctions than the other two ads. Over the next hour, the algorithm showed the first ad, which featured a photo of colorful Hubble boxes against a blue background, to more and more users; the algorithm had begun to favor it, apparently. As Rosen refreshed his browser, the sensation was like watching a seed sprout. The ad got more views. Some led to clicks. And eventually, sometime between 11:28 a.m. and 11:53 a.m., one of those clicks led to the test's first sale. Commerce was in bloom.

The moment felt odd. Obviously there was science behind the scenes; the algorithm was a set of rules written by Facebook engineers. But from where Rosen sat, the operation might as well have been run by the Holy Spirit. Facebook's artificial-intelligence algorithm had wound its way through the server farms, reached out among two billion users, found an individual and showed her a Hubble ad on Instagram — and she used her credit card to buy a subscription for contact lenses.

In quick succession, the first ad generated two more sales. The algorithm started increasing how much it bid on Hubble's behalf, thus winning even more auctions for ad space and spending more of Hubble's money on it — first $1 a minute, then $2 a minute, then more than

$3. By 2 p.m., Facebook's A.I. had charged Hubble $306.50 to put that ad in front of 9,684 users. The second ad, after an outlay of $8.03, had been all but abandoned. And the third ad was hardly given a chance: Since 8 a.m., it had appeared before only 30 people.

"No idea why," Rosen said, shaking his head. Rosen could see all sorts of data arranged in neat rows on Facebook's Ads Manager program: the number of views, clicks, sales and the average cost, in advertising, of acquiring each new customer. But none of the metrics at Rosen's fingertips could resolve a fundamental mystery: why the algorithm behaved as it did, why it preferred some ads over others and why the third ad got little attention whatsoever.

The morning's ads were incredibly similar: "hubblecontacts," the company's Instagram handle, appeared at the top, above pictures of boxes in peach, blue, yellow and green. The only differences were that the first ad showed the boxes of contact lenses lined up against a blue background; in the second and third ads, they were set against a split pink-and-blue background and were arranged diagonally in the second and scattershot in the third. But they were all just boxes! Did Instagram users really prefer contact-lens ads with strict rows of boxes or blue backgrounds? Had rules been written into the algorithm favoring orderly arrangements? (The Hubble team knew Facebook favored certain aesthetics.) To what extent was the day's outcome, apparently set in motion when the first ad happened to get that first click in the morning, actually random? Rosen could only guess.

Advertising has always been an uncertain business. No one has ever known why, exactly, some people respond to an ad in a newspaper or a spot on TV, much less why specific individuals decide to buy products when they do. (The oldest cliché in the ad world, usually attributed to the department-store magnate John Wanamaker: "Half my advertising is wasted. The trouble is, I don't know which half.") But to make money in advertising, you don't have to be all-knowing; your ads simply need to work better than those of a competitor. To this end, advertisers inevitably pursue some combination of two major approaches. They test and refine their messages, trying to craft one as efficient and targeted as possible (junk-mailers of preapproved credit-card offers, for example). Or they showboat, putting on a huge spectacle that's sure to attract someone (Super Bowl advertisers).

In the early 2010s, direct-to-consumer companies showboated. But lacking the money for big TV ad campaigns, they relied instead on old-fashioned public relations, panache and luck. Warby Parker hired a public-relations firm to pitch its concept to Vogue and GQ and debuted its website on the same day issues reached subscribers. It also held an event featuring bespectacled models at the New York Public Library during Fashion Week. Dollar Shave Club first succeeded on account of the exquisite timing, both commercial and comedic, of its founder, Michael Dubin. He made a funny, low-budget video introducing his company, then uploaded it to YouTube on the same day TechCrunch reported Dollar Shave Club's first round of venture funding. Within days, after some immediate attention at the South by Southwest festival in Austin, Tex., Dubin had three million views online.

Facebook's sales pitch — putting the right ad in front of the right person, thanks to the wonders of data technology — isn't exactly new. As far back as 1964, William Allan, a business editor for The Pittsburgh Press, reported that in the near future, "computers will tell business-men which half of their advertising budgets are being wasted." Thirty years later, The Economist described an effort to take advantage of American Express's transactional records: "Powerful data-crunching computers known as massive parallel processors, equipped with neural-network software (which searches, like the human brain, for patterns in a mass of data), hold out a vision of marketing nirvana." Companies like Acxiom, Experian and Datalogix have been offering similar data-mining services to direct marketers for years. What sets Facebook (and Google) apart are scale and sophistication.

A recent study by a Princeton professor, Arvind Narayanan, and a doctoral candidate, Steven Englehardt, provides a sense of how thoroughly the two online giants monitor user behavior. In early 2016, they examined the top one million websites in the world, using special bots they developed to scour them for tracking mechanisms. Google had trackers on 76 percent of these sites, Facebook on 23 percent of them. (Twitter, in third place, had trackers on just over 12 percent of the sites.) The tech giants can examine all this data looking for patterns and then match them back to prospective customers.

What also sets Facebook and Google apart from their direct-marketing forebears is that they give access to everyday advertisers. Anyone with a credit card can go online and test ads on Facebook's platform, one of the most sophisticated direct-marketing operations ever. But while average people can use the machine, there's still a lot of mystery about how it works. The methods and calculations of the algorithm — why it ends up pushing some ads and not others — are all hidden.

Almost as soon as they began, Rosen, Horwitz and the others at Hubble became determined to fathom the algorithm's secrets — to figure out why some ads succeeded and others didn't. Soon they were trading hypotheses with other entrepreneurs, cribbing ideas from other companies' ads and taking a formal approach to testing, rooted in the scientific method. They uploaded ads with identical images but different wordings, for example. The Hubble team wound up concluding all sorts of things. Ads with third-party endorsements — from GQ, say, or BuzzFeed — beat those with their own slogans. Ads featuring close-ups of the Hubble boxes outperformed those with human models. Ads that included a button that said "Shop Now" or "Learn More" fared worse than an ad with no button at all; viewers simply preferred to click anywhere on the picture to go to the website.

But even as the Hubble team gleaned more about what yielded successful Facebook ads, the algorithm could be unpredictable, almost moody. If you kept loading the same ads into the same ad set every day, they stopped performing as well. The founders figured at first that users were tiring of the same ads. But actual viewer numbers revealed that practically no individual user had seen any ad more than once. The algorithm itself seemed to grow bored. At night, meanwhile, the algorithm spent lots of money and rarely found customers. The Hubble executives started shrinking the budgets at 11 p.m., which they called "putting the algorithm to bed." The algorithm could also be impulsive and streaky — some days it might go on a sudden jag, blowing a thousand dollars in a few hours with nothing to show for it. At any time, any one of the 15 different ad sets might go haywire. Rosen found himself checking the Ads Manager compulsively on his laptop and his iPhone. (Facebook offers an iOS app for advertisers.) "It occupies my brain constantly," he says. "It's that feeling of 'Did you leave the oven on?' "

One night we went to a standup-comedy night Rosen hosted at a bar called Muchmore's in Brooklyn. (For the past four years, he has moonlighted as a comedian.) But while the other comics were onstage, Rosen was on the Ads Manager the whole time. "Who cares about jokes?" he quipped afterward.

Eager for help, Rosen sought guidance from a former Facebook employee named Faheem Siddiqi, who now runs his own marketing agency. Hubble's sales representative at Facebook told him that Siddiqi had figured out the best ways to optimize Facebook advertising campaigns. But it turned out that Siddiqi and his employees checked the Ads Manager even more compulsively than Rosen — every half-hour, for up to 16 hours a day. When I asked Siddiqi to share his tips for managing Facebook ads, he replied, "Step 1 is meditation."

"It's like a baby," Jesse Horwitz told me. "If you go more than half an hour without checking in on it, it's probably dead." (Horwitz, who is married, does not yet have children.)

Middlemen — creative agencies, media planners, publishers — have long ruled the advertising business. Yet until recently they have not been as omnipresent, opaque and inhuman as Facebook. The social giant now dictates, more fully and precisely than ever before, which ads we see and who sees which ads. Some of the implications of this are amusing, others troubling.

In my house, the strange new world of advertising announced itself in the form of a water pitcher. The Soma 6-Cup Pitcher is a paragon of

Brooklynite beauty: folksy oak handle, sleek minimalist reservoir, filter cones made out of coconut shells (or something). I had never heard of it before my wife ordered one online. Plenty of my friends hadn't, either. When our visitors opened the fridge, half of them were like me: Soma ignorant. The other half knew the brand immediately: *Hey! You got a Soma?* They had seen the pitcher on Facebook, on Instagram, all over the place. What was a familiar brand to some was totally unknown to me and others. We had been divvied up. It's something I've noticed again and again: I see an ad for Aaptiv, a running app; my wife sees ads for a furniture website called Article that I've still never visited. Just as Facebook steers conservative and liberal talking points to users who already share those perspectives, we're being sorted into commercial bubbles as well.

Recently ProPublica, the investigative-journalism nonprofit, showed how bad actors can abuse this process: Facebook's software gave advertisers the option to target "Jew Haters," for instance. In a separate investigation, ProPublica found that Facebook made it possible to exclude specific "ethnic affinities" from seeing ads, noting that ads excluding people based on race are prohibited by federal housing and employment laws.

This stereotyping isn't a glitch of Facebook's machine-learning process — it's how the software works. To formulate audiences, the algorithm scours profiles and analyzes them for shared traits and correlations and self-identified interests and, it assumes, our preferences, grouping us into tribes that can be targeted. It's up to Facebook and advertisers to constrain this amoral process in ethical and lawful ways. Yet the ethics of targeting are not clear-cut. In May, The Australian reported that Facebook employees had prepared a document showing how they could gather details on teenagers during vulnerable moments — when Facebook users feel "stressed," "insecure," "defeated" or "worthless." Is that immoral, or simply crass?

Such challenges are opening a new front for companies and corporate-responsibility watchdogs. Bad human actors don't pose the only problem; a machine-learning algorithm, left unchecked, can misbehave and compound inequality on its own, no help from humans needed. The same mechanism that decides that 30-something women who like yoga disproportionately buy Lululemon tights — and shows them ads for more yoga wear — would also show more junk-food ads to impoverished populations rife with diabetes and obesity.

"Sometimes data behaves unethically," Antonio Garcia-Martinez, a former Facebook employee who worked on the advertising team, wrote in an essay in The Guardian. He provided an example from his time at the company: "Someone on the data-science team had cooked up a new tool that recommended Facebook pages users should like. And what did this tool start spitting out? Every ethnic stereotype you can imagine."

As algorithms sort users in increasingly complex ways — already the multivaried criteria for determining a Lookalike group defies human comprehension — regulators and companies will have to confront how to determine who is being nudged, and why, and whether that's benefiting the public or exacerbating societal ills. An algorithm that draws its lessons from the present reality can't be counted on to improve the course of the future on its own.

Facebook's A.I. isn't operating unattended, certainly: Garcia-Martinez wrote that Facebook decided not to release the recommendation tool. Facebook points out that it makes efforts to prevent harmful advertising. It does not, for instance, allow ads for payday loans, which prey on the poor. It says it has removed advertisers' ability to target users by ethnicity when promoting housing, employment or credit; it removed "Jew Haters" and other objectionable categories and said it would increase human review of its ad-targeting options. In response to the report in The Australian, Facebook said the analysis "was intended to help marketers understand how people express themselves on Facebook. It was never used to target ads."

Yet managing a platform this way — seeing what mischief the algorithm and its users gets up to, then responding with countermeasures — can be difficult to sustain. "This is a whack-a-mole problem, one among many Facebook has," Garcia-Martinez told me. It makes Facebook, a company still largely controlled by a single man, Mark Zuckerberg, the ultimate arbiter of morality and taste for all two billion of its users. It also means the company has unilateral power to make or break companies when it tweaks its system.

This is not a hypothetical possibility. In 2013, media sites like those measured by the BuzzFeed Partner network, which includes BuzzFeed, Thought Catalog and The New York Times, noticed a huge surge in referrals from Facebook — a jump of more than 50 million page views from August to October. A year later, Facebook announced that it had adjusted its news-feed algorithm to eliminate so-called click bait. Upworthy, a peddler of stories with headlines like "9 Out of 10 Americans Are Completely Wrong About This Mind-Blowing Fact," had its total page views decline by half in the span of three months, from 90 million to 48 million visitors. (At the time of these huge shifts, 30 percent of Americans got news from Facebook. In 2017, 45 percent of Americans do, according to Pew Research Center.)

"We always knew that Facebook is sort of like the weather," says Eli Pariser, Upworthy's co-founder and president. "There's going to be sunny days and stormy days." In response to the algorithm adjustment, Pariser instructed his staff to stop posting as many videos to YouTube, which is owned by Google, and start publishing more videos directly to Facebook instead.

"That certainly served Facebook well," Pariser admits. "But you know, I also wouldn't be able to reach 200 million people on any other medium," he says, citing the reach of Upworthy's videos on Facebook. The platform may be mercurial, but Upworthy still relies on it.

Imagine, now, that Facebook tweaks its algorithm in a way that — rather than cause wild swings in web traffic to a purveyor of viral videos — leads to a steep decline in advertising and sales for a consumer-products company, one that happens to be the largest employer in a small town. Or imagine multiple companies shaken up by such an adjustment, or an entire industry overhauling its practices to suit Facebook. Even the threat and uncertainty of those possibilities could hurt businesses, which depend on predictable returns to invest in future projects.

As we delegate more control to artificial intelligence, both businesses as well as users are venturing into uncertain territory. In the meantime, more and more companies — start-ups, mom-and-pop stores, major corporations — are handing their dollars and their data to the social-networking giant. Facebook's Ads Manager is user-friendly. Sales are plentiful. And if you don't take advantage of it, your competitors will. How could you not go there?

By mid-March, a few weeks after I first followed Rosen, the Hubble team no longer had 15 Facebook and Instagram ad sets. It had 40 — all pointed at discrete audiences, each with its own handful of ads. But Rosen looked more rested, less frazzled. He explained that he and Paul Rodgers had developed something they called "Robo-Dan," a few lines of code that checked the Ads Manager every hour, then adjusted the budget as Rosen would. He could wake up and let the ads run (although he had to fight the compulsion to check on Robo-Dan). Soon, he told me, they would upgrade to Robo-Dan 2, which would switch in new ads, taking over the nightly bedtime routine. (With 40 audiences, he told me, going through the process lasted almost as long as an entire episode of "The Late Show With Stephen Colbert.") Finally, he said, he was getting some distance from Facebook's everyday machinations. Someday soon, he would be able to go to bed early, he told me. Or have an evening to himself.

But by the end of June, Rosen's stress-free life was still a dream. A new problem arose: No matter what new ads they put in an ad set, the growth rate of sales declined and the cost per acquisition went up. They began to think it was an audience problem: Had they found all the customers in those groups? With their ad sets going fallow, the Hubble team scrambled to find fresh and fertile ground. Their ideas for new audiences got quirkier, more outlandish. One week they zeroed in on people who like Sweetgreen, the salad chain. Next they went after people who had indicated that they were fans of bottled water, whoever they are. Each group fizzled after a few days — the cost per each new customer climbed higher and higher; sales dwindled. As they searched for more and more audience descriptors, they landed upon a novel idea: They began trading their Lookalike groups with other online retailers, figuring that the kind of people who buy one product from social media will probably buy others. This sort of audience sharing is becoming more common on Facebook: There is even a company, TapFwd, that pools together Lookalike groups for various brands, helping them show ads to other groups.

Cogan and Horwitz have decided that they need to reduce their dependence on Facebook advertising, for the sake of their business and their own sanity. In May, they tested their first 15-second cable-television commercials. With TV, the data is vaguer, and it takes longer to get results back. Yet even though the old medium provides them with less information than Facebook, in some ways the ignorance is bliss. "There's fewer levers; there's less to stress out about." Rodgers says. "You can push the button and get on with your life."

In August, the Hubble team finally handed over their domestic Facebook advertising work to an outside agency, Ampush, that charges them based on how many new customers sign up. Ten people at Ampush now do the job of Rosen and Robo-Dan. Still, the handoff was bittersweet. "We ran their numbers — it's something we could beat," Rosen says, meaning Hubble could get more customers for less money if it did the ad buying in-house. "But it would destroy our lives."

Thanks largely to Facebook, Hubble is on track to finish its first full year in business having made $20 million in revenue. In August, Hubble raised $10 million, valuing the company at $210 million. In January, Hubble will use those funds to expand its business to Continental Europe. Its advertising strategy? Robo-Dan, with some help from Rosen. As Hubble advances into new territories, Facebook and the algorithm will be tagging along with them.

BURT HELM is a senior contributing writer for Inc. magazine. This is his first article for The New York Times Magazine.

CHAPTER 4

Media Pivots and Conspiracy Cranks: The Power of Video

As traditional print media digitized and reoriented to the profits of web traffic, video emerged as a significant presence. Bolstered by the popularity of YouTube, many publishers began a well-publicized "pivot to video," prioritizing video production over articles. And yet, unforeseen issues emerged in the video economy, especially problems in the market for children's videos. Likewise, many found that YouTube algorithms led to massive profits for conspiracy theorists and far-right extremists.

Why That Video Went Viral

BY NATALIE KITROEFF | MAY 19, 2014

THERE IT WAS, virtual gold: a video of a firefighter resuscitating a kitten trapped in a smoky home.

Neetzan Zimmerman, then an editor at Gawker, a news and gossip site, knew it was destined for viral magic. But before he could publish a post about it, his editor made a request. Mr. Zimmerman was to include the epilogue omitted by most every other outlet: The kitten died of smoke inhalation soon after being saved.

For telling the whole story, Mr. Zimmerman paid a price.

"That video did tremendously well for practically everyone who posted it," he recalled, "except Gawker."

Why should one sad detail mean the difference between an online megahit and a dud? What makes content go viral?

Social sharing is powerful enough to topple dictatorships and profitable enough to merit multibillion-dollar investments. But scientists are only beginning to explore the psychological motivations that turn a link into "click bait" and propel a piece of content to Internet fame.

Their research may have significant implications for the media and advertising businesses, whose profits hinge on winning the cutthroat race for the attention of Internet users worldwide. Already, some notions of the ingredients in this modern alchemy are beginning to emerge.

If you want to melt the Internet, best to traffic in emotion, researchers have found. The emotional response can be happy or sad, but the more intense it is, the more likely the story is to be passed along.

In a study led by Rosanna Guadagno, a social psychologist at the University of Texas at Dallas, 256 participants much preferred to forward a funny video than one of a man treating his own spider bite. But they were likely to share any video that evoked an intense emotional response, Dr. Guadagno found.

Similarly, Jonah Berger and Katherine Milkman, professors at the Wharton School at the University of Pennsylvania, have found that uplifting articles are more likely than disheartening ones to land on the most-emailed list at The New York Times. But even stories evoking rage or other negative, strong emotions are emailed by readers more often than ones that are simply depressing.

"People share things they have strong emotional reactions to, especially strong positive reactions," Dr. Guadagno said.

Sharing is not just how information ripples across communities; it's also how emotions are disseminated. Recently, analysts at Facebook, Yale and the University of California, San Diego, reviewed more than a billion posts by Facebook users, and found that when users vented on a rainy day, their friends in other cities posted bleak status updates more frequently than normal.

But positive status updates were even more contagious, prompting upbeat updates from friends at even greater rates. The conclusion: Online, as in real life, feelings can be caught like the flu.

The most shared post at Upworthy, a site for shareable content, is a video about a boy who died of cancer, but not before producing a hit song and performing sold-out shows. The post has racked up nearly 20 million views, thanks in part to the type of methodically calculated headline that has become the site's trademark: "This Amazing Kid Got to Enjoy 19 Awesome Years on This Planet. What He Left Behind Is Wondtacular."

"Even though it was a really sad story, it was a story that gave you something to do with that sadness," said Upworthy's analytics czar, Daniel Mintz.

For many people, sharing seems to be a way to process the highs and lows they feel while consuming content online. Mr. Berger, who studied the Times articles, conducted a follow-up study in which he instructed one group of students to jog in place for 60 seconds before going online, while a comparison group rested before logging on.

The runners were more than twice as likely as the sedentary group to email the same article, he found. Why? Because they were already physiologically aroused, Mr. Berger theorizes, and forwarding or liking something serves as a form of release.

"Arousal is an aversive state, so people want to get out of it by sharing," Mr. Berger said. Misery loves company, and so does any sort of deeply affecting feeling.

But pressing the share button can also be driven by ego. Constructing and refining an online persona has become a daily task for many, experts say; posting a link that evokes laughter or gasps can confer status on the sharer.

No surprise, then, that data recently compiled by Chartbeat, a company that measures online traffic, suggests that people often post articles on Twitter that they haven't actually read.

"What we found is that there is no relationship whatsoever with the amount that the article is shared and the amount of engaged time and attention given to that article," said Tony Haile, Chartbeat's chief executive.

Like a bookshelf stocked with classic tomes that have never been opened, the links that adorn Facebook walls and Twitter accounts are markers of the people we aspire to be. And online media companies are increasingly aware that their role is to package content that will make each member of the masses who disseminates it burnish an online reputation while feeling, oddly, unique.

Mr. Zimmerman, formerly of Gawker, saw it as his job to help the reader feel like "that guy who is always plugged in and tapped into what's going on."

"People build their online identities by sharing," he said. "They want people to think of them a certain way."

YouTube Kids App Faces New Complaints Over Ads for Junk Food

BY CECILIA KANG | NOV. 24, 2015

WASHINGTON — Visit YouTube Kids and typically it will not be long before promotions for junk food appear. The advertisements regularly show up in the form of funny contests and animated stories.

In complaints filed to federal officials on Tuesday, two prominent consumer advocacy groups argued that those ads were deceptive, particularly for children. The two complaints, made to the Federal Trade Commission, expand on the groups' filings to the agency in April and could increase pressure on federal officials to intervene in the fast-growing online video market.

The groups, the Campaign for a Commercial-Free Childhood and the Center for Digital Democracy, argue in the complaints that online video aimed at children is too commercialized and is not held to the same standards that apply to cable and broadcast television. The complaints call for an investigation of food marketers, video programmers and Google, which owns YouTube, as well as for a broad examination of advertising of such food to children online.

"You have digital natives consuming content simultaneously with the growth of powerful marketing at children at the earliest ages," said Jeffrey Chester, executive director of the Center for Digital Democracy. "The agencies are lagging and the companies are emboldened."

Google introduced YouTube Kids in February as a mobile app "built from the ground up with little ones in mind," according to a blog post by the company. The app is geared for children of preschool age and older. After downloading the app on a mobile device, parents are guided through a tour of how to set safety features, like the option to block searching. The videos on the platform are selected from the main YouTube site through algorithms set to pick child-related content.

The groups expand on their April complaints by asking the F.T.C. to examine the advertising practices of food companies, and by citing new evidence of junk food ads on the app. In the new complaint, the groups argue that more than a dozen food companies have fallen short of their own promises to abstain from marketing junk food to children on YouTube Kids. The groups say that brands like Burger King, Coca-Cola, ConAgra Foods and American Licorice have commercials on the app for products including potato chips and chocolate bars.

While the groups direct blame toward marketers, they also criticize YouTube for not enforcing its own policies. YouTube restricts paid advertising of food and beverages on its children's app, but the groups said their review of the app found many examples in which food companies used their own branded channels to show promotional videos. The groups asked for an investigation into uploaded TV commercials from unknown YouTube Kids accounts to determine whether there were connections between the food companies and those channels.

The Federal Trade Commission has been reviewing the April complaint, according to a person with knowledge of the investigation who spoke on the condition of anonymity. The F.T.C. usually accepts complaints and begins at least a preliminary review process.

Any investigation of the previous complaint and the new filings would not be public, said Jessica Rich, director of the Bureau of Consumer Protection at the F.T.C. "We welcome and we review carefully all such complaints submitted to us," she added.

The Children's Food and Beverage Advertising Initiative, a coalition of major food and beverage companies that is mentioned in the complaint, said it had complied with its commitments. The organization said the companies did not place food ads on YouTube Kids, but it had seen how their ads could appear via the search function. The group said it had asked Google to find a technology fix to prevent the ads from appearing there.

The group's "participants are not purchasing advertisements on the YouTube Kids app, even for foods that meet C.F.B.A.I.'s nutrition criteria," it said in a statement.

For children's television programming, there are clear rules that limit the length of commercials, as well as restrictions on product placement and on the promotion of products by TV hosts and characters. The Children's Food and Beverage Advertising Initiative, formed in 2006, promised not to advertise any products that did not meet certain nutritional standards to children under 12 on TV or online.

YouTube Kids states in its parental guide that it cannot be responsible for user-generated content by branded channels or third parties.

YouTube said last week that the app had been downloaded more than 10 million times and had received strong ratings in app stores.

The company said parents could turn off the search function to help block content they do not want to reach their children. YouTube said on Tuesday that it had not seen the complaints, but a spokeswoman said, "We are always open to feedback and are committed to creating the best experience for families."

The lines between marketing and advertising are often blurred, the groups said in their complaint. They asked the F.T.C. to investigate what appeared to be promotional videos by YouTube creators and said the agency should enforce its disclosure rules on paid sponsorships.

"There is just so much commercial content, and more of it all the time," said Angela Campbell, a professor at Georgetown Law School and an author of the complaints. "And if they are trying to sell something, they aren't making it obvious even to an adult. So to a kid, that is fundamentally unfair."

On YouTube Kids, Startling Videos Slip Past Filters

BY SAPNA MAHESHWARI | NOV. 4, 2017

IT WAS A TYPICAL NIGHT in Staci Burns's house outside Fort Wayne, Ind. She was cooking dinner while her 3-year-old son, Isaac, watched videos on the YouTube Kids app on an iPad. Suddenly he cried out, "Mommy, the monster scares me!"

When Ms. Burns walked over, Isaac was watching a video featuring crude renderings of the characters from "PAW Patrol," a Nickelodeon show that is popular among preschoolers, screaming in a car. The vehicle hurtled into a light pole and burst into flames.

The 10-minute clip, "PAW Patrol Babies Pretend to Die Suicide by Annabelle Hypnotized," was a nightmarish imitation of an animated series in which a boy and a pack of rescue dogs protect their community from troubles like runaway kittens and rock slides. In the video Isaac watched, some characters died and one walked off a roof after being hypnotized by a likeness of a doll possessed by a demon.

"My initial response was anger," said Ms. Burns, a nurse, who credits the app with helping Isaac to learn colors and letters before other boys his age. "My poor little innocent boy, he's the sweetest thing, and then there are these horrible, horrible, evil people out there that just get their kicks off of making stuff like this to torment children."

Parents and children have flocked to Google-owned YouTube Kids since it was introduced in early 2015. The app's more than 11 million weekly viewers are drawn in by its seemingly infinite supply of clips, including those from popular shows by Disney and Nickelodeon, and the knowledge that the app is supposed to contain only child-friendly content that has been automatically filtered from the main YouTube site.

But the app contains dark corners, too, as videos that are disturbing for children slip past its filters, either by mistake or because bad actors have found ways to fool the YouTube Kids algorithms.

In recent months, parents like Ms. Burns have complained that their children have been shown videos with well-known characters in violent or lewd situations and other clips with disturbing imagery, sometimes set to nursery rhymes. Many have taken to Facebook to warn others, and share video screenshots showing moments ranging from a Claymation Spider-Man urinating on Elsa of "Frozen" to Nick Jr. characters in a strip club.

Malik Ducard, YouTube's global head of family and learning content, said that the inappropriate videos were "the extreme needle in the haystack," but that "making the app family friendly is of the utmost importance to us."

While the offending videos are a tiny fraction of YouTube Kids' universe, they are another example of the potential for abuse on digital media platforms that rely on computer algorithms, rather than humans, to police the content that appears in front of people — in this case, very young people.

And they show, at a time when Congress is closely scrutinizing technology giants, how rules that govern at least some of the content on children's television fail to extend to the digital world.

When videos are uploaded to YouTube, algorithms determine whether or not they are appropriate for YouTube Kids. The videos are continually monitored after that, Mr. Ducard said, a process that is "multilayered and uses a lot of machine learning." Several parents said they expected the app to be safer because it asked during setup whether their child was in preschool or older.

Mr. Ducard said that while YouTube Kids may highlight some content, like Halloween videos in October, "it isn't a curated experience." Instead, "parents are in the driver's seat," he said, pointing to the ability to block channels, set usage timers and disable search results.

Parents are also encouraged to report inappropriate videos, which someone at YouTube then manually reviews, he said. He noted that in the past 30 days, "less than .005 percent" of the millions of videos viewed in the app were removed for being inappropriate.

Staci Burns, who lives near Fort Wayne, Ind., said her "initial response was anger" when she saw one of her sons watching a disturbing video on YouTube Kids.

"We strive," he added, "to make that fraction even lower."

Holly Hart of Gray, Tenn., said she was recently reading while her 3-year-old daughter was in the room when she noticed that Disney Junior characters in the video her daughter was watching started "turning into monsters and trying to feed each other to alligators." An image previewing a recommended video showed the characters in a provocative pose.

"It was an eye-opener for me," said Ms. Hart, who had downloaded the app because it was being used at the local elementary school.

Not all of the inappropriate videos feature cartoons. Alisa Clark Wilcken of Vernal, Utah, said her 4-year-old son had recently seen a video of a family playing roughly with a young girl, including a scene in which her forehead is shaved, causing her to wail and appear to bleed.

Most of the videos flagged by parents were uploaded to YouTube in recent months by anonymous users with names like Kids Channel TV and Super Moon TV. The videos' titles and descriptions feature popular character names and terms like "education" and "learn colors."

They are independently animated, presumably to avoid copyright violations and detection. Some clips uploaded as recently as August have millions of views on the main YouTube site and run automatically placed ads, suggesting they are financially lucrative for the makers as well as YouTube, which shares in ad revenue. It is not clear how many of those views came on YouTube Kids.

One video on YouTube Kids from the account Subin TV shows the "PAW Patrol" characters in a strip club. One of them then visits a doctor and asks for her cartoon legs to be replaced with long, provocative human legs in stilettos. The account's description says, "Video created with the purpose of learning and development of children!"

The account that posted the video seen by Ms. Burns's son is named Super Ares TV and has a Facebook page called PAW Patrol Awesome TV. Questions sent there were mostly ignored, though the account did reply: "That's a Cute character and video is a funny story, take it easy, that's it."

The Super Ares TV account seems to be linked to a number of other channels targeting children with cartoon imitations, based on their similar channel fonts, animation style and Greek mythology-inspired names, from Super Hermes TV and Super Apollo TV to Super Hera TV.

A Super Zeus TV account included a link to a shopping site called SuperKidsShop.com, which is registered in Ho Chi Minh City, Vietnam. A call to the phone number listed in that site's registration records was answered by a man who declined to identify himself. He said that his partners were responsible for the videos and that a team of about 100 people worked on them. He said he would forward email requests for comment to them. Those emails went unanswered.

Dr. Michael Rich, a pediatrics professor at Harvard Medical School and the director of the Center on Media and Child Health, said such videos brought up a host of issues for children. "It's just made that much more upsetting by the fact that characters they thought they knew and trusted are behaving in these ways," he said.

Josh Golin, executive director of the Campaign for a Commercial-Free Childhood, argued that inappropriate videos on YouTube Kids showed hazards of today's media reality.

"Algorithms are not a substitute for human intervention, and when it comes to creating a safe environment for children, you need humans," Mr. Golin said. His group and the Center for Digital Democracy filed a complaint with the Federal Trade Commission in 2015 accusing YouTube Kids of deceptive marketing to parents based on inappropriate videos.

Using automation for online advertising has turned Google into a behemoth worth more than half a trillion dollars. The company has faced a new wave of criticism in the past year for lacking human oversight after its systems inadvertently funded fake news sites and hateful YouTube videos and most likely sold election-related ads to accounts affiliated with the Russian government.

Google has largely defended its errors by pointing to the enormous amount of content it hosts, including more than 400 hours of content uploaded to YouTube every minute.

Disney and Nickelodeon, mainstays of children's programming, work with YouTube Kids to introduce children to their characters. But they are also aware that their content can be mixed in with disturbing knockoffs.

"Nickelodeon creates its characters and shows to entertain kids, so we share the same concern as parents about the unsuitable nature of some of the videos being served to them," said David Bittler, a spokesman for the Viacom-owned network.

A Disney spokesman said YouTube Kids had assured the company that it was "working on ways to more effectively and proactively prevent this type of situation from occurring."

Some parents have taken to deleting the app. Others, like Ms. Burns, still allow its use, just on a more limited, supervised basis.

"This is a children's application — it's targeted to children," said Crissi Gilreath, a mother of two in Oklahoma, "and I just can't believe that with such a big company they don't have people whose job it is to filter and flag."

What the 'Pivot to Video' Looks Like at Condé Nast

BY VALERIYA SAFRONOVA | APRIL 4, 2018

IT TOOK THREE MEN two hours to shoot a 63-second overhead instructional video of Laura Rege, a recipe developer, making a cake for Bon Appétit — what people in the food-video industry call a "hands and pans."

At the Kitchen Studio, Condé Nast's new 7,000-square-foot space in Industry City in Brooklyn, four to six of these "hands and pans" videos are shot daily. It is the type of video on which Tasty, BuzzFeed's famous recipe offshoot, has built a very large audience. Condé Nast's food brands, Bon Appétit and Epicurious, have heartily embraced the format too.

Now, the company wants to double its current video business. To do so, it will have to move beyond what's worked in the age of Facebook video, and make something new.

A LESS WASTEFUL CONDÉ NAST

Until now, most of Condé Nast's food videos were made in its test kitchen in the company's headquarters at One World Trade Center or in Airbnb rentals. But business has been growing. Over the last two years, Bon Appétit's YouTube subscriber base increased from 34,000 to more than 1 million. In the same period, the number of monthly unique viewers for the videos on its website grew by nearly 2.5 million, according to comScore. Over all, video now makes up a quarter of revenue for The Lifestyle Collection — that's Bon Appétit, Architectural Digest, Epicurious, Condé Nast Traveler and the now digital-only publication Self. All told, these brands produce about 40 to 50 videos per week, and that doesn't include those made for advertisers.

At the same time, the company expected significant overall revenue decline from 2016 to 2017. It closed the print edition of Teen Vogue; reduced the print frequency of GQ, Architectural Digest and Glamour; and cut employees across the company. After that crusade of downsizing — and the turnover of big-spending old-guard editors in chief like Vanity Fair's former editor Graydon Carter — there are now rumors of the impending departure of Anna Wintour, the company's artistic director and the editor of Vogue. "We emphatically deny these rumors," a spokesman told Page Six this week. She has unexpectedly become the avatar of a right-sized, moderately thrifty Condé Nast.

And, rightly or not, Condé Nast is finally looking to digital. In recent years, it has launched additional online verticals; introduced a platform for gay, lesbian and transgender issues called "them"; and embraced digitally focused leaders like Samantha Barry, the new editor in chief of Glamour, and Phillip Picardi, the chief content officer of Teen Vogue.

Perhaps not surprisingly, a significant portion of the company's advertising solicitation is now devoted to video.

The idea that video will be a financial savior in the media business is contentious, and often mocked. It is expensive to create, and audiences aren't equivalent — yet — to print or even web in their ability to be monetized. (In human terms: One person watching a video is not financially equivalent to what one person paying for a magazine has been worth.)

But Vogue the magazine has just over a million paid subscriptions, and Vogue the YouTube channel has more than 2.2 million subscribers.

"In the next 24 months, I hope that video is half our business," said Craig Kostelic, the chief business officer of The Lifestyle Collection. "It's critical. It's the macro trend of content consumption."

PEOPLE LIKE TO WATCH PEOPLE, NOT FINGERS

Condé Nast is not betting everything on "hands and pans" videos. In fact, it is increasingly looking beyond them as viewers gravitate toward something that is a cross between short social videos and the food programs of yore (you might remember it as cable television). Much of the space is for videos featuring hosts like Claire Saffitz, who is known for videos in which she breaks down complex recipes for foods as varied

Carla Lalli Music, the food director of Bon Appétit, makes scallops in the Condé Nast test kitchen.

as Twinkies and soup dumplings, or Brad Leone, the quirky host of "It's Alive," a series about fermentation, pickling and more.

"For so long we were doing those hands and pans videos, and it's one of those things you had to do based on internet demand and traffic," said Adam Rapoport, the editor in chief of Bon Appétit. "They're kind of boring, they're not stimulating and they're predictable. It was not creatively rewarding. As an industry, we've gone beyond that and it's gone more to the personality videos, to more narrative."

Bon Appétit has attracted hundreds of thousands of viewers with human-first series like one in which children react to various foods, for example breakfast items from the last hundred years ("the beginning is horrible, so is the middle, so I'll give it a four," said one sophisticated taster about a 1920s breakfast of codfish cakes, hominy and stewed prunes), or another where the magazine's deputy editor swaps out his office for 24 hours of hands-on labor at fast-paced casual restaurants like Katz's deli in New York (he is critiqued by one of his temporary co-workers for being "a little too nice"). Epicurious, while much smaller (it has about 146,000 YouTube subscribers) has similarly attracted audiences with video series like the 50 Person Prep Challenge, in which people attempt basic culinary tasks like slicing a pepper or dicing an onion.

PRODUCTS, PLACED

To optimize the new test kitchens for filming, they have been outfitted with overhead lights, blackout curtains and acoustic paneling to muffle outside sound. All the stovetops are gas. "People want to see the flame," said Eric Gillin, the digital general manager of The Lifestyle Collection. Sponsored product is everywhere. The countertops? Caesarstone. The small appliances? Braun. Furniture? Crate & Barrel. The smart fridges? Samsung. And so on.

And though the test kitchen at Condé Nast's headquarters has served well as a shooting location, it will now go back to being primarily a work space for editors who are trying out recipes. "Video can be kind of intrusive," said Mr. Rapoport. "You have camera people, lights, you have to section off a portion of the kitchen, you don't want people to be too noisy. Shooting interrupts the basic workflow."

A FAREWELL TO FACEBOOK

"On YouTube, over half of our audience is under 34 years old. These people are young, they're really engaged, they're watching for an average of over five minutes. It's not this 8-second watch time like on Facebook," said Matt Duckor, the executive producer for the Lifestyle Collection.

"YouTube is a sneaky, over-the-top kind of channel unto itself," Mr. Gillin said.

Videos that are somewhere between the length of a social media post and a 60-minute special thrive on YouTube, Mr. Duckor said. A significant chunk of viewers are consuming them not on a cellphone or computer but on a television. "Twenty percent of people watched that cheesesteak video on a television, whether on a smart TV, a game console, Roku or

Apple TV," Mr. Duckor said, referring to a video in which a Bon Appétit editor ate 16 Philly cheesesteaks in 12 hours. "Coming across something in your Facebook feed and stopping on it for three seconds can count as a view, but when we talk to advertisers, they want people who are actually connecting with what they're doing, not just happening upon it."

The Condé Nast teams have embraced the flexibility of the mid-length format. "When you're post-cable, it's not a half-hour TV show, you're not programming for these ad blocks, you're telling the story for as long as there's a story to be told," Mr. Gillin said.

"This industry is moving so fast," Mr. Duckor said. "The videos we're creating now compared to two years ago are really different, but you're always going to need kitchens, you're always going to need the ability to have production space to have people work and sit."

WHAT'S AN AD NOW?

For now, the revenue coming in from videos is split between advertising and sponsorships. "About half to two-thirds of it is more about traditional ads, like pre-roll," Mr. Kostelic said, referring to the brief advertisements that play before a video. But increasingly Condé Nast makes videos for its clients that it does not promote on its own platforms.

"Historically, you would have a digital media plan with a set amount of view or impressions," Mr. Kostelic said. "More people are coming to us for our content and creative services plans, with distribution being a separate conversation."

The greater goal is for the lessons the Lifestyle Collection team will learn with the Kitchen Studio space to trickle out to the rest of the company.

"The issue that Condé Nast used to have is that it was really siloed out by brand, and the brands didn't speak to each other, they didn't share learnings," Mr. Duckor said. "We're at a place now where we can take learnings from Bon Appétit and the success we've had on YouTube and apply them to Architectural Digest, where they haven't quite had the investment in that platform that we have. That's the real opportunity."

As Germans Seek News, YouTube Delivers Far-Right Tirades

COLUMN | BY MAX FISHER AND KATRIN BENNHOLD | SEPT. 7, 2018

CHEMNITZ, GERMANY — The day after far-right demonstrators took over the streets here, Sören Uhle, a city official who oversees municipal marketing and development, began to get strange phone calls from reporters.

The man whose killing had set off the riots, they said, had died while trying to stop asylum seekers from molesting a local woman. And it wasn't just one local man who had been killed, but two. Could he comment?

These sorts of accusations suddenly seemed to be everywhere. But none were true. They had come, Mr. Uhle and others suspected, from social media — particularly YouTube.

Ray Serrato, a Berlin-based digital researcher, noticed the tide of misinformation when his wife's uncle showed him a YouTube video that claimed the rioters had been Muslim refugees.

The video, posted by an obscure fringe group, was rambling, and it appeared to be cheaply produced. Yet it had nearly half a million views — far more than any news video on the riots. How was that possible?

Mr. Serrato scraped YouTube databases for information on every Chemnitz-related video published this year. He found that the platform's recommendation system consistently directed people toward extremist videos on the riots — then on to far-right videos on other subjects.

Users searching for news on Chemnitz would be sent down a rabbit hole of misinformation and hate. And as interest in Chemnitz grew, it appears, YouTube funneled many Germans to extremist pages, whose view counts skyrocketed.

Activists say this may have contributed to a flood of misinformation, helping extremists shape public perceptions even after they had been run off Chemnitz's streets.

"This was new," Mr. Uhle said. "It's never happened to me before that mainstream media, big German newspapers and television channels, ask me about false news and propaganda that had clearly become so pervasive that people just bought it."

Researchers who study YouTube say the episode, far from being isolated, reflects the platform's tendency to push everyday users toward politically extreme content — and, often, to keep them there.

A YouTube spokeswoman declined to comment on the accusations, saying the recommendation system intended to "give people video suggestions that leave them satisfied." She said the company planned to work with news publishers to help "build a better news experience on YouTube."

Though YouTube has typically drawn less scrutiny than other social networks, that may be changing. Its parent company, Google, faced criticism from American lawmakers this week for declining to send its chief executive to congressional hearings attended by chief executives from Twitter and Facebook.

A CLOSED SYSTEM

YouTube's recommendation system is the core of its business strategy: Getting people to click on one more video means serving them more ads. The algorithm is sophisticated, constantly learning what keeps users engaged. And it is powerful. A high ranking from the algorithm can mean huge audiences for a video.

Mr. Serrato wondered if that explained how his family member had discovered the conspiracy video. He had read studies about users who blindly followed the recommendation system; inevitably, they seemed to end up watching long series of far-left or far-right videos.

Zeynep Tufekci, a prominent social media researcher at the University of North Carolina at Chapel Hill, has written that these findings suggest that YouTube could become "one of the most powerful radicalizing instruments of the 21st century."

But, as Ms. Tufekci and other researchers stress, such experiments are anecdotal.

Mr. Serrato wanted to get a fuller picture of how YouTube shapes perceptions of events. So he conducted something known as a network analysis, applying techniques he had used in his day job, as an analyst with Democracy Reporting International, a respected global governance monitor, to track hate speech in Myanmar.

Using YouTube's public developer interface, Mr. Serrato plugged in a dozen recent videos related to Chemnitz. For each, he scraped YouTube's recommendations for what to watch next. Then he did the same for those videos, and so on. Eventually, he identified a network of about 650 videos, nearly all from this year.

The results, he said, were disturbing. The network showed a tight cluster of videos that Mr. Serrato identified as predominantly conspiracy theorist or far right.

This was the first sign that YouTube's algorithm systemically directs users toward extremist content. A more neutral algorithm would most likely produce a few distinct clusters of videos — one of mainstream news coverage, another of conspiracy theories, another of extremist groups. Those who began in one cluster would tend to stay there.

Instead, the YouTube recommendations bunched them all together, sending users through a vast, closed system composed heavily of misinformation and hate.

Viewers who come to YouTube for down-the-middle news may quickly find themselves in a world of extremists, Mr. Serrato said.

"That's what I found bizarre," he said. "Why are they so close together, unless the aim is to trigger a reaction?" Content that engages viewers' emotions or curiosity, he suspected, would hook them in. And it wasn't just that the platform directed people to unreliable videos about the subject they had sought out — in this case, Chemnitz.

Many of the videos in Mr. Serrato's analysis were unrelated to Chemnitz. Some offered positive portrayals of white nationalism in general or of Alternative for Germany, a far-right political party.

Others went further astray, detailing fringe conspiracies; one argues that President Trump is a pawn of the Rothschild banking family.

Why would YouTube surface videos like these in a search for news stories?

How many steps are there on YouTube's algorithm from news story to fever swamp? "Only two," Mr. Serrato said. "By the second, you're quite knee-deep in the alt-right."

Perhaps most striking is what was absent. The algorithm rarely led back to mainstream news coverage, or to liberal or centrist videos on Chemnitz or any other topic. Once on the fringes, the algorithm tended to stay there, as if that had been the destination all along.

FROM FRINGE TO MAINSTREAM

Activists and residents in Chemnitz say far-right conspiracy theories seemed unusually common in the days before and after the demonstration.

Oliver Flesch, a far-right figure on YouTube, posted a series of videos misrepresenting the killing that set off the riots, with titles like "German Stabbed to Death Just Because He Wanted to Help Our Women." Another claimed the asylum seekers had killed two Germans.

Mr. Flesch, who has 20,000 subscribers, operates in a political bubble. Yet his claims had filtered into the mainstream enough that journalists asked Mr. Uhle, the Chemnitz official, about them. How?

The algorithm may have helped. Mr. Serrato's network analysis led to 16 of Mr. Flesch's videos, and to five by the obscure right-wing rapper Chris Ares, with whom Mr. Flesch sometimes does guest spots.

And misinformation can travel in other ways. Some German officials said this week that a widely circulated video, appearing to show a far-right activist chasing a dark-skinned person during Chemnitz's riots, may have been faked.

Thomas Hoffmann, who helps run a local refugee organization, was on a train from Hamburg when the riots broke out. So he searched YouTube for "Chemnitz" and the date, hoping to follow the events.

Instead, the platform returned obvious forgeries. One video of dark-skinned residents being attacked was edited to make them look like the aggressors. Others were interspersed with footage from previous rallies, to make this one look more peaceful than it was.

"It was incredible how much blatantly doctored material there was," Mr. Hoffmann said. "When you click on one video, whether you like it or not, another one is proposed that features content from far-right conspiracy theories."

IS YOUTUBE WORSE THAN OTHERS?

YouTube has been more cooperative with the German authorities about removing hate speech than other social media companies, said Flemming Ipsen, who tracks political extremism at Jugendschutz.net, a government-linked internet monitor.

But some researchers consider YouTube to be unusually permissive about content that it does not consider overt hate speech, and its algorithm unusually aggressive in pushing users toward political fringes. YouTube also designates some content as borderline, neither blocking nor promoting it.

YouTube says it does not code videos by political content, but rather by viewer interest. Critics say that leads the platform to surface fringe material that reliably wins more clicks.

Mr. Serrato said that even while researching videos he found abhorrent, he was unable to resist.

"As soon as I was on one of the videos, I thought, O.K., now I'm going to watch the next one," he said. "That's YouTube's goal. I stay engaged, ads play. And it works."

Guillaume Chaslot, a former engineer at YouTube's owner, Google, said that during and after high-profile political events like the demonstration in Chemnitz, extremism and misinformation often spike on the platform. But this reflects deeper tendencies in YouTube's algorithm, he said.

"The example I like to cite is the flat-earth theory, because it's apolitical," Mr. Chaslot said. Videos claiming the earth is flat, he said, are "still going viral, still getting highly recommended by the YouTube algorithm, because it gets watch time."

Mr. Chaslot worked on YouTube's algorithm until 2013, when he was fired. Google has said he was fired for poor performance, Mr. Chaslot has cited disagreements over the company's direction.

Now, he studies the algorithm from outside, most recently analyzing its recommendations during the 2016 presidential campaign. As in Chemnitz, he found that YouTube's suggestions consistently nudged users into extremist content.

"YouTube doesn't give you a straight representation of the world," Mr. Chaslot said. "It looks like reality, but it deforms reality, because it is biased toward watch time."

Even in Germany, which has some of the toughest social media restrictions of any democracy, officials say they have little power to regulate the vast majority of social media content.

"Lies, propaganda and manipulation are harmful for society, but on their own are not illegal — and so our hands are often tied," said Mr. Ipsen, of the government-linked internet monitor.

German officials have urged social media companies to make their algorithms more transparent. American lawmakers have done the same, citing research linking social media to polarization, foreign meddling and hate speech.

But the companies are refusing.

"The algorithm is central to their business model," Mr. Ipsen said. "All we can do is remind them of their social responsibility."

The Interpreter is a column by **MAX FISHER** and **AMANDA TAUB** exploring the ideas and context behind major world events.

CHRISTOPHER F. SCHUETZE contributed reporting from Berlin.

New Pressure on Google and YouTube Over Children's Data

BY SAPNA MAHESHWARI | SEPT. 20, 2018

IN THE CONTEXT of a growing national debate on tech and privacy, Google has come under increased scrutiny for how it may be tracking and targeting children for advertising.

Two House members sent a letter this week to the company's chief executive, Sundar Pichai, expressing concern that the collection practices of YouTube, a Google subsidiary, may not comply with the Children's Online Privacy Protection Act, known as Coppa.

The letter on Monday — from David Cicilline, Democrat of Rhode Island, and Jeff Fortenberry, Republican of Nebraska — followed up on a complaint filed in April by more than 20 advocacy groups. The groups sought an investigation by the Federal Trade Commission, which enforces Coppa.

In addition to the complaint and the lawmakers' letter, Google is facing pressure from the New Mexico attorney general on how it may collect children's location data. The state official named the tech giant as a defendant in a lawsuit filed last week against the developer of Fun Kid Racing and other gaming apps, along with advertisers involved with them, claiming that they were sharing children's data without their parents' permission.

YouTube has said its practices are in line with Coppa, which requires companies to obtain explicit, verifiable permission from parents before collecting personal information from children under 13 or targeting them with ads tied to their online behavior.

"There's more interest in children's privacy than there has been in a long time, and that's related to the broader privacy conversations that we're having," said Josh Golin, executive director of the Campaign for a Commercial-Free Childhood, who was involved with the

April complaint and the new push by lawmakers. "Whether that leads to Google being held to account is yet to be seen."

YouTube's terms of service state that its main app and website are meant only for viewers 13 and older, which means that the site does not have to comply with Coppa. The company directs those under 13 to the YouTube Kids app, which pulls its videos from the main site. Google's website says YouTube Kids prohibits "interest-based advertising" and ads with "tracking pixels."

But advocates have contended that YouTube is aware that plenty of children watch videos on the main site, and Representatives Cicilline and Fortenberry are pressing Google to provide details of how it may collect data from children's videos on the site.

"In light of the kind of content that is on YouTube focused on attracting young users, it raises serious questions about what efforts are being made to make sure that information is not being collected about children and mined and sold," Mr. Cicilline said.

Google, the biggest seller of online advertising, said its policies did not allow advertisers to deliver personalized ads to children under 13 or collect their personal information.

"We're committed to protecting children online with a combination of family-friendly products and strict policies," a Google spokeswoman said in a statement.

Several of the most-viewed channels on YouTube are aimed at children, including ChuChu TV and Ryan ToysReview, according to Social Blade, which compiles social media data. The channels, according to the site, have attracted billions of views. That's good for ad revenue, which YouTube splits with video makers.

Mr. Golin said he was disappointed that the Federal Trade Commission, which met with children's rights advocates in May after they filed their complaint, hadn't acted on the issue. Lawmakers and the New Mexico attorney general "are really stepping up and putting pressure on the companies that should be coming from the F.T.C.," he added.

Still, Mr. Golin said he was optimistic that the congressmen could glean information from Google.

"These are not questions we've ever gotten answers to, and it would be great to get on the record what Google and YouTube actually know about this," he said.

The Federal Trade Commission declined to comment.

The letter from the two lawmakers concludes with a series of pointed questions that ask Google to explain how it determines the age of its users, whether or not it collects the same personal data from children and adults and why YouTube includes channels that are "clearly child-directed."

Mr. Cicilline and Mr. Fortenberry gave Google a deadline of Oct. 17 to reply.

YouTube Unleashed a Conspiracy Theory Boom. Can It Be Contained?

COLUMN | BY KEVIN ROOSE | FEB. 19, 2019

LAST MONTH, THE YouTube star Shane Dawson uploaded his new project: a 104-minute documentary, "Conspiracy Theories With Shane Dawson."

In the video, set to a spooky instrumental soundtrack, Mr. Dawson unspooled a series of far-fetched hypotheses. Among them: that iPhones secretly record their owners' every utterance; that popular children's TV shows contain subliminal messages urging children to commit suicide; that the recent string of deadly wildfires in California was set on purpose, either by homeowners looking to collect insurance money or by the military using a type of high-powered laser called a "directed energy weapon."

None of this was fact-based, of course, and some of the theories seemed more like jokey urban legends than serious accusations. Still, his fans ate it up. The video has gotten more than 30 million views, a hit even by Mr. Dawson's standards. A follow-up has drawn more than 20 million views and started a public feud with Chuck E. Cheese's, the restaurant chain, which was forced to deny claims that it recycles customers' uneaten pizza slices into new pizzas.

Mr. Dawson's conspiracy series arrived at a particularly awkward moment for YouTube, which has been reckoning with the vast troves of misinformation and extreme content on its platform.

In late January, the company announced that it was changing its recommendations algorithm to reduce the spread of "borderline content and content that could misinform users in harmful ways." It cited, as examples, "videos promoting a phony miracle cure for a serious illness, claiming the earth is flat or making blatantly false claims about historic events like 9/11."

Mr. Dawson, whose real name is Shane Lee Yaw, has more than 20 million subscribers and a devoted teenage fan base. He has built his lucrative career by, among other talents, understanding what kinds of content plays well on YouTube.

For years, that meant conspiracy theories — lots and lots of them, all delivered with the same wide-eyed credulity. In a 2016 video, he wondered aloud if the first Apollo moon landing was staged by NASA. ("It's a theory," he said, "but, I mean, all the evidence is not looking good.") In 2017, he discussed the false theory that the attacks of Sept. 11, 2001, were a hoax. ("I know it's crazy," he said, "but just look at some of these videos.") And last year, he devoted a segment of a video to flat-earth theory, which he concluded "kind of makes sense."

In fairness, Mr. Dawson is a far cry from partisan cranks like Alex Jones, the Infowars founder, who was barred by YouTube and other social networks last year for hate speech. Most of Mr. Dawson's videos have nothing to do with conspiracies, and many are harmless entertainment.

But the popularity of Mr. Dawson's conspiracy theories illuminates the challenge YouTube faces in cleaning up misinformation. On Facebook, Twitter and other social platforms, the biggest influencers largely got famous somewhere else (politics, TV, sports) and have other vectors of accountability. But YouTube's stars are primarily homegrown, and many feel — not entirely unreasonably — that after years of encouraging them to build their audiences with viral stunts and baseless rumor-mongering, the platform is now changing the rules on them.

Innocent or not, Mr. Dawson's videos contain precisely the type of viral misinformation that YouTube now says it wants to limit. And its effort raises an uncomfortable question: What if stemming the tide of misinformation on YouTube means punishing some of the platform's biggest stars?

A representative for Mr. Dawson did not respond to a request for comment. A YouTube spokeswoman, Andrea Faville, said: "We recently announced that we've started reducing recommendations

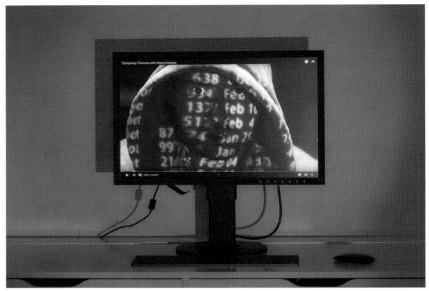

COREY OLSEN FOR THE NEW YORK TIMES

of borderline content or videos that could misinform users in harmful ways. This is a gradual change and will get more and more accurate over time."

Part of the problem for platforms like YouTube and Facebook — which has also pledged to clean up misinformation that could lead to real-world harm — is that the definition of "harmful" misinformation is circular. There is no inherent reason that a video questioning the official 9/11 narrative is more dangerous than a video asserting the existence of U.F.O.s or Bigfoot. A conspiracy theory is harmful if it results in harm — at which point it's often too late for platforms to act.

Take, for example, Mr. Jones's assertion that the mass shooting at Sandy Hook Elementary School in 2012 was a hoax perpetrated by gun control advocates. That theory, first dismissed as outrageous and loony, took on new gravity after Mr. Jones's supporters began harassing the grieving parents of victims.

Or take Pizzagate, a right-wing conspiracy theory that alleged that Hillary Clinton and other Democrats were secretly running a child-

138 FILTER BUBBLES AND TARGETED ADVERTISING

sex ring. The theory, which was spread in a variety of videos on You-Tube and other platforms, might have remained an internet oddity. But it became a menace when a believer showed up at a pizza restaurant in Washington, D.C., with an assault rifle, vowing to save the children he believed were locked in the basement.

To its credit, YouTube has taken some minor steps to curb misinformation. Last year, it began appending Wikipedia blurbs to videos espousing certain conspiracy theories, and changed the way it handles search results for breaking news stories so that reliable sources are given priority over opportunistic partisans. And last summer, it was among the many social networks to bar Mr. Jones and Infowars.

In a multipart Twitter thread this month, Guillaume Chaslot, a former YouTube software engineer, called the company's decision to change its recommendation algorithm a "historic victory."

Mr. Chaslot noted that this algorithm — which was once trained to maximize the amount of time users spend on the site — often targeted vulnerable users by steering them toward other conspiracy theory videos it predicts they will watch.

The change "will save thousands from falling into such rabbit holes," he wrote.

In an interview last week, Mr. Chaslot was more circumspect, saying YouTube's move may have amounted to a "P.R. stunt." Because the change will affect only which videos YouTube recommends — conspiracy theories will still show up in search results, and they will still be freely available to people who subscribe to the channels of popular conspiracy theorists — he called it a positive but insufficient step.

"It will address only a tiny fraction of conspiracy theories," he said.

Last year, Mr. Chaslot built a website, AlgoTransparency.org, to give outsiders a glimpse of YouTube's recommendation algorithms at work. The site draws from a list of more than 1,000 popular YouTube channels, and calculates which videos are most often recommended to people who watch those channels' videos.

On many days, conspiracy theories and viral hoaxes top the list. One recent day, the most frequently recommended video was "This Man Saw Something at Area 51 That Left Him Totally Speechless!," which was recommended to viewers of 138 channels. The second most recommended video, which linked a series of recent natural disasters to apocalyptic prophecies from the Book of Revelation, was recommended to viewers of 126 of those top channels.

In our conversation, Mr. Chaslot suggested one possible solution to YouTube's misinformation epidemic: new regulation.

Lawmakers, he said, could amend Section 230 of the Communications Decency Act — the law that prevents platforms like YouTube, Facebook and Twitter from being held legally liable for content posted by their users. The law now shields internet platforms from liability for all user-generated content they host, as well as the algorithmic recommendations they make. A revised law could cover only the content and leave platforms on the hook for their recommendations.

"Right now, they just don't have incentive to do the right thing," Mr. Chaslot said. "But if you pass legislation that says that after recommending something 1,000 times, the platform is liable for this content, I guarantee the problem will be solved very fast."

But even new laws governing algorithmic recommendations wouldn't reverse the influence of YouTube celebrities like Mr. Dawson. After all, many of his millions of views come from his fans, who subscribe to his channel and seek out his videos proactively.

YouTube's first challenge will be defining which of these videos constitute "harmful" misinformation, and which are innocent entertainment meant for an audience that is largely in on the joke.

But there is a thornier problem here. Many young people have absorbed a YouTube-centric worldview, including rejecting mainstream information sources in favor of platform-native creators bearing "secret histories" and faux-authoritative explanations.

When those creators propagate hoaxes and conspiracy theories as part of a financially motivated growth strategy, it seeps in with some percentage of their audience. And sometimes — in ways no algorithm could predict — it leads viewers to a much darker place.

It's possible that YouTube can still beat back the flood of conspiracy theories coursing through its servers. But doing it will require acknowledging how deep these problems run and realizing that any successful effort may look less like a simple algorithm tweak, and more like deprogramming a generation.

KEVIN ROOSE is a columnist for Business and a writer-at-large for The New York Times Magazine. His column, The Shift, examines the intersection of technology, business and culture.

CHAPTER 5

Political Uses of the Personalized Web

Though the Internet was used in politics well before 2016, that election year changed digital campaigns. Conservatives charged Facebook with bias in its algorithms, sparking a debate about neutrality in web platforms. Meanwhile, advertising revenue made partisan posting — regardless of its truthfulness — lucrative across the political spectrum, leading to the phenomenon of "fake news." Most alarmingly, people used consumer data to directly market inflammatory political ads appealing to users' individual biases, transforming how elections are conducted.

Facebook's Bias Is Built-In, and Bears Watching

COLUMN | BY FARHAD MANJOO | MAY 11, 2016

FACEBOOK IS THE WORLD'S most influential source of news.

That's true according to every available measure of size — the billion-plus people who devour its News Feed every day, the cargo ships of profit it keeps raking in, and the tsunami of online traffic it sends to other news sites.

But Facebook has also acquired a more subtle power to shape the wider news business. Across the industry, reporters, editors and media executives now look to Facebook the same way nesting baby chicks look to their engorged mother — as the source of all knowledge and nourishment, the model for how to behave in this scary new-media world. Case in point: The New York Times, among others, recently began an initiative to broadcast live video. Why do you suppose that might be? Yup, the F word. The deal includes payments from Facebook to news outlets, including The Times.

Yet few Americans think of Facebook as a powerful media organization, one that can alter events in the real world. When blowhards rant about the mainstream media, they do not usually mean Facebook, the mainstreamiest of all social networks. That's because Facebook operates under a veneer of empiricism. Many people believe that what you see on Facebook represents some kind of data-mined objective truth unmolested by the subjective attitudes of fair-and-balanced human beings.

None of that is true. This week, Facebook rushed to deny a report in Gizmodo that said the team in charge of its "trending" news list routinely suppressed conservative points of view. Last month, Gizmodo also reported that Facebook employees asked Mark Zuckerberg, the social network's chief executive, if the company had a responsibility to "help prevent President Trump in 2017." Facebook denied it would ever try to manipulate elections.

Even if you believe that Facebook isn't monkeying with the trending list or actively trying to swing the vote, the reports serve as timely reminders of the ever-increasing potential dangers of Facebook's hold on the news. That drew the attention of Senator John Thune, the Republican of South Dakota who heads the Senate's Commerce Committee, who sent a letter on Tuesday asking Mr. Zuckerberg to explain how Facebook polices bias.

The question isn't whether Facebook has outsize power to shape the world — of course it does, and of course you should worry about that power. If it wanted to, Facebook could try to sway elections, favor certain policies, or just make you feel a certain way about the world, as it once proved it could do in an experiment devised to measure how emotions spread online.

There is no evidence Facebook is doing anything so alarming now.

The danger is nevertheless real. The biggest worry is that Facebook doesn't seem to recognize its own power, and doesn't think of itself as a news organization with a well-developed sense of institutional ethics and responsibility, or even a potential for bias. Neither does its audience, which might believe that Facebook is immune to bias because it is run by computers.

That myth should die. It's true that beyond the Trending box, most of the stories Facebook presents to you are selected by its algorithms, but those algorithms are as infused with bias as any other human editorial decision.

"Algorithms equal editors," said Robyn Caplan, a research analyst at Data & Society, a research group that studies digital communications systems. "With Facebook, humans are never not involved. Humans are in every step of the process — in terms of what we're clicking on, who's shifting the algorithms behind the scenes, what kind of user testing is being done, and the initial training data provided by humans."

Mark Zuckerberg, the Facebook chief. The company says it would never try to manipulate elections.

Everything you see on Facebook is therefore the product of these people's expertise and considered judgment, as well as their conscious and unconscious biases apart from possible malfeasance or potential corruption. It's often hard to know which, because Facebook's editorial sensibilities are secret. So are its personalities: Most of the engineers, designers and others who decide what people see on Facebook will remain forever unknown to its audience.

Facebook also has an unmistakable corporate ethos and point of view. The company is staffed mostly by wealthy coastal Americans who tend to support Democrats, and it is wholly controlled by a young billionaire who has expressed policy preferences that many people find objectionable. Mr. Zuckerberg is for free trade, more open immigration and for a certain controversial brand of education reform. Instead of "building walls," he supports a "connected world and a global community."

You could argue that none of this is unusual. Many large media outlets are powerful, somewhat opaque, operated for profit, and controlled by wealthy people who aren't shy about their policy agendas — Bloomberg News, The Washington Post, Fox News and The New York Times, to name a few.

But there are some reasons to be even more wary of Facebook's bias. One is institutional. Many mainstream outlets have a rigorous set of rules and norms about what's acceptable and what's not in the news business.

"The New York Times contains within it a long history of ethics and the role that media is supposed to be playing in democracies and the public," Ms. Caplan said. "These technology companies have not been engaged in that conversation."

According to a statement from Tom Stocky, who is in charge of the trending topics list, Facebook has policies "for the review team to ensure consistency and neutrality" of the items that appear in the trending list.

But Facebook declined to discuss whether any editorial guidelines governed its algorithms, including the system that determines what people see in News Feed. Those algorithms could have

profound implications for society. For instance, one persistent worry about algorithmic-selected news is that it might reinforce people's previously held points of view. If News Feed shows news that we're each likely to Like, it could trap us into echo chambers and contribute to rising political polarization. In a study last year, Facebook's scientists asserted the echo chamber effect was muted.

But when Facebook changes its algorithm — which it does routinely — does it have guidelines to make sure the changes aren't furthering an echo chamber? Or that the changes aren't inadvertently favoring one candidate or ideology over another? In other words, are Facebook's engineering decisions subject to ethical review? Nobody knows.

The other reason to be wary of Facebook's bias has to do with sheer size. Ms. Caplan notes that when studying bias in traditional media, scholars try to make comparisons across different news outlets. To determine if The Times is ignoring a certain story unfairly, look at competitors like The Washington Post and The Wall Street Journal. If those outlets are covering a story and The Times isn't, there could be something amiss about The Times's news judgment.

Such comparative studies are nearly impossible for Facebook. Facebook is personalized, in that what you see on your News Feed is different from what I see on mine, so the only entity in a position to look for systemic bias across all of Facebook is Facebook itself. Even if you could determine the spread of stories across all of Facebook's readers, what would you compare it to?

"Facebook has achieved saturation," Ms. Caplan said. No other social network is as large, popular, or used in the same way, so there's really no good rival for comparing Facebook's algorithmic output in order to look for bias.

What we're left with is a very powerful black box. In a 2010 study, Facebook's data scientists proved that simply by showing some users that their friends had voted, Facebook could encourage people to go to the polls. That study was randomized — Facebook wasn't selectively showing messages to supporters of a particular candidate.

But could it? Sure. And if it happens, you might never know.

State of the Art is a column from **FARHAD MANJOO** that examines how technology is changing business and society.

Facebook's Subtle Empire

OPINION | BY ROSS DOUTHAT | MAY 21, 2016

IN ONE STORY people tell about the news media, we have moved from an era of consolidation and authority to an era of fragmentation and diversity. Once there were three major television networks, and everyone believed what Walter Cronkite handed down from Sinai. Then came cable TV and the talk radio boom, and suddenly people could seek out ideologically congenial sources and tune out the old mass-culture authorities. Then finally the Internet smashed the remaining media monopolies, scattered news readers to the online winds, and opened an age of purely individualized news consumption.

How compelling is this story? It depends on what you see when you look at Facebook.

In one light, Facebook is a powerful force driving fragmentation and niche-ification. It gives its users news from countless outlets, tailored to their individual proclivities. It allows those users to be news purveyors in their own right, playing Cronkite every time they share stories with their "friends." And it offers a platform to anyone, from any background or perspective, looking to build an audience from scratch.

But seen in another light, Facebook represents a new era of media consolidation, a return of centralized authority over how people get their news. From this perspective, Mark Zuckerberg's empire has become an immensely powerful media organization in its own right, albeit one that effectively subcontracts actual news gathering to other entities (this newspaper included). And its potential influence is amplified by the fact that this Cronkite-esque role is concealed by Facebook's self-definition as "just" a social hub.

These two competing understandings have collided in the last few weeks, after it was revealed that Facebook's list of "trending topics" is curated by a group of toiling journalists, not just an impersonal algorithm, and after a former curator alleged that decisions about which stories "trend" are biased against conservative perspectives.

This news outraged some conservatives, but others shrugged. After Zuckerberg summoned a collection of right-of-center mavens to his Silicon Valley throne room — er, boardroom — for an airing of grievances, one of the participants, Glenn Beck, criticized his fellow conservatives for treating Facebook like a left-wing monolith, rather than an open platform that has served many conservatives (himself included) very well.

To which Ben Domenech, author of the popular conservative newsletter The Transom, retorted that Facebook is obviously not just an open platform, that its curation of the news automatically makes it an important gatekeeper as well, and that it's therefore "an act of foolishness or cowardice" to fail to hold displays of bias to account.

Who's right? Well, Beck is right that Facebook is different in kind from any news organization before it, and that traditional critiques of media bias — from the Chomskyite left as well as from the right — don't apply neatly to what it's doing.

Between the algorithmic character of (much of) its news dissemination, the role of decentralized user choice, and the commercial imperatives of personalization, there's little chance that the Facebook experience will ever bear the kind of ideological stamp that, say, the Time-Life empire bore in Henry Luce's heyday.

But Domenech is right that Zuckerberg's empire still needs vigilant watchdogs and rigorous critiques. True, any Facebook bias is likely to be subtler-than-subtle. But because so many people effectively live *inside* its architecture while online, there's a power in a social network's subtlety that no newspaper or news broadcast could ever match.

In a period of crisis, that subtle power could be exercised in truly disturbing ways: Consider, for instance, the reported conversation at a Facebook meeting about whether the company might have an obligation to intervene against a figure like Donald Trump — something that a tweak of its news algorithm or even its Election Day notification could theoretically help accomplish.

But the more plausible (and inevitable) exercise of Facebook's power would be basically unconscious — as, I suspect, any suppression of conservative stories may have been.

Human nature being what it is, a social network managed and maintained by people who tend to share a particular worldview — left-libertarian and spiritual-but-not-religious, if I judge the biases of Silicon Valley right — will tend to gently catechize its users into that perspective.

And of course this runs deeper than politics. The way even an "impersonal" algorithm is set up, the kind of stories it elevates and buries, is also a form of catechesis, a way of teaching human beings about how they should think about the world.

Virtual architecture tells stories no less than the real variety: Like stained-glass windows in a medieval cathedral, even what seem like offhand choices — like Google's choice of its Doodle subject, to cite a different new media entity — point people toward particular icons, particular ideals.

So even if you don't particularly care how Facebook treats conservative news sources, you should still want its power constantly checked, critiqued and watched — for the sake not just of its users' politics, but their very selves and souls.

ROSS DOUTHAT is an Op-Ed columnist for The New York Times.

Inside Facebook's (Totally Insane, Unintentionally Gigantic, Hyperpartisan) Political-Media Machine

BY JOHN HERRMAN | AUG. 24, 2016

How a strange new class of media outlet has arisen to take over our news feeds.

OPEN YOUR FACEBOOK FEED. What do you see? A photo of a close friend's child. An automatically generated slide show commemorating six years of friendship between two acquaintances. An eerily on-target ad for something you've been meaning to buy. A funny video. A sad video. A recently live video. Lots of video; more video than you remember from before. A somewhat less-on-target ad. Someone you saw yesterday feeling blessed. Someone you haven't seen in 10 years feeling worried.

And then: A family member who loves politics asking, "Is this really who we want to be president?" A co-worker, whom you've never heard talk about politics, asking the same about a different candidate. A story about Donald Trump that "just can't be true" in a figurative sense. A story about Donald Trump that "just can't be true" in a literal sense. A video of Bernie Sanders speaking, overlaid with text, shared from a source you've never seen before, viewed 15 million times. An article questioning Hillary Clinton's honesty; a headline questioning Donald Trump's sanity. A few shares that go a bit too far: headlines you would never pass along yourself but that you might tap, read and probably not forget.

Maybe you've noticed your feed becoming bluer; maybe you've felt it becoming redder. Either way, in the last year, it has almost certainly become more intense. You've seen a lot of media sources you don't recognize and a lot of posts bearing no memorable brand at all. You've seen politicians and celebrities and corporations weigh in directly; you've probably seen posts from the candidates themselves. You've seen people you're close to and people you're not, with increasing levels of urgency, declare it is now time to speak up, to take a stand, to set aside allegiances or hangups or political correctness or hate.

Facebook, in the years leading up to this election, hasn't just become nearly ubiquitous among American internet users; it has centralized online news consumption in an unprecedented way. According to the company, its site is used by more than 200 million people in the United States each month, out of a total population of 320 million. A 2016 Pew study found that 44 percent of Americans read or watch news on Facebook. These are approximate exterior dimensions and can tell us only so much. But we can know, based on these facts alone, that Facebook is hosting a huge portion of the political conversation in America.

The Facebook product, to users in 2016, is familiar yet subtly expansive. Its algorithms have their pick of text, photos and video produced and posted by established media organizations large and small, local and national, openly partisan or nominally unbiased. But there's also a new and distinctive sort of operation that has become hard to miss: political news and advocacy pages made specifically for Facebook, uniquely positioned and cleverly engineered to reach audiences exclusively in the context of the news feed. These are news sources that essentially do not exist outside of Facebook, and you've probably never heard of them. They have names like Occupy Democrats; The Angry Patriot; US Chronicle; Addicting Info; RightAlerts; Being Liberal; Opposing Views; Fed-Up Americans; American News; and hundreds more. Some of these pages have millions of followers; many have hundreds of thousands.

Using a tool called CrowdTangle, which tracks engagement for Facebook pages across the network, you can see which pages are most shared, liked and commented on, and which pages dominate the conversation around election topics. Using this data, I was able to speak to a wide array of the activists and entrepreneurs, advocates and opportunists, reporters and hobbyists who together make up 2016's most disruptive, and least understood, force in media.

Individually, these pages have meaningful audiences, but cumulatively, their audience is gigantic: tens of millions of people. On Facebook, they rival the reach of their better-funded counterparts in the political media, whether corporate giants like CNN or The New York Times, or openly ideological web operations like Breitbart or Mic. And unlike traditional media organizations, which have spent years trying to figure out how to lure readers out of the Facebook ecosystem and onto their sites, these new publishers are happy to live inside the world that Facebook has created. Their pages are accommodated but not actively courted by the company and are not a major part of its public messaging about media. But they are, perhaps, the purest expression of Facebook's design and of the incentives coded into its algorithm — a system that has already reshaped the web and has now inherited, for better or for worse, a great deal of America's political discourse.

In 2006, when Mark Zuckerberg dropped out of college to run his rapidly expanding start-up, Mark Provost was a student at Rogers State University in Claremore, Okla., and going through a rough patch. He had transferred restlessly between schools, and he was taking his time to graduate; a stock-picking hobby that grew into a promising source of income had fallen apart. His outlook was further darkened by the financial crisis and by the years of personal unemployment that followed. When the Occupy movement began, he quickly got on board. It was only then, when Facebook was closing in on its billionth user, that he joined the network.

Now 36, Provost helps run US Uncut, a left-leaning Facebook page and website with more than 1.5 million followers, about as many as MSNBC has, from his apartment in Philadelphia. (Sample headlines: "Bernie Delegates Want You to See This DNC Scheme to Silence Them" and "This Sanders Delegate Unleashing on Hillary Clinton Is Going Absolutely Viral.") He frequently contributes to another popular page, The Other 98%, which has more than 2.7 million followers.

Occupy got him on Facebook, but it was the 2012 election that showed him its potential. As he saw it, that election was defined by social media. He mentioned a set of political memes that now feel generationally distant: Clint Eastwood's empty chair at the 2012 Republican National Convention and Mitt Romney's debate gaffe about "binders full of women." He thought it was a bit silly, but he saw in these viral moments a language in which activists like him could spread their message.

Provost's page now communicates frequently in memes, images with overlaid text. "May I suggest," began one, posted in May 2015, when opposition to the Trans-Pacific Partnership was gaining traction, "the first 535 jobs we ship overseas?" Behind the text was a photo of Congress. Many are more earnest. In an image posted shortly thereafter, a photo of Bernie Sanders was overlaid with a quote: "If Germany, Denmark, Sweden and many more provide tuition-free college," read the setup, before declaring in larger text, "we should be doing the same." It has been shared more than 84,000 times and liked 75,000 more. Not infrequently, this level of zeal can cross into wishful thinking. A post headlined "Did Hillary Clinton Just Admit on LIVE TV That Her Iraq War Vote Was a Bribe?" was shared widely enough to merit a response from Snopes, which called it "quite a stretch."

This year, political content has become more popular all across the platform: on homegrown Facebook pages, through media companies with a growing Facebook presence and through the sharing habits of users in general. But truly Facebook-native political pages have begun to create and refine a new approach to political news: cherry-picking and reconstituting the most effective tactics and tropes from activism, advocacy and journalism into a potent new mixture. This strange new class of media organization slots seamlessly into the news feed and is especially notable in what it asks, or doesn't ask, of its readers. The point is not to get them to click on more stories or to engage further with a brand. The point is to get them to share the post that's right in front of them. Everything else is secondary.

While web publishers have struggled to figure out how to take advantage of Facebook's audience, these pages have thrived. Unburdened of any allegiance to old forms of news media and the practice, or performance, of any sort of ideological balance, native Facebook page publishers have a freedom that more traditional publishers don't: to engage with Facebook purely on its terms. These are professional Facebook users straining to build media companies, in other words, not the other way around.

From a user's point of view, every share, like or comment is both an act of speech and an accretive piece of a public identity. Maybe some people want to be identified among their networks as news junkies, news curators or as some sort of objective and well-informed reader. Many more people simply want to share specific beliefs, to tell people what they think or, just as important, what they don't. A newspaper-style story or a dry, matter-of-fact headline is adequate for this purpose. But even better is a headline, or meme, that skips straight to an ideological conclusion or rebuts an argument.

Rafael Rivero is an acquaintance of Provost's who, with his twin brother, Omar, runs a page called Occupy Democrats, which passed three million followers in June. This accelerating growth is attributed by Rivero, and by nearly every left-leaning page operator I spoke with, not just to interest in the election but especially to one campaign in particular: "Bernie Sanders is the Facebook candidate," Rivero says. The rise of Occupy Democrats essentially mirrored the rise of Sanders's primary run. On his page, Rivero started quoting text from Sanders's frequent email blasts, turning them into Facebook-ready memes with a consistent aesthetic: colors that pop, yellow on black. Rivero says that it's clear what his audience wants. "I've probably made 10,000 graphics, and it's like running 10,000 focus groups," he said. (Clinton was and is, of course, widely discussed by Facebook users: According to the company, in the last month 40.8 million people "generated interactions" around the candidate. But Rivero says that in the especially engaged, largely oppositional left-wing-page ecosystem, Clinton's message and cautious brand didn't carry.)

Because the Sanders campaign has come to an end, these sites have been left in a peculiar position, having lost their unifying figure as well as their largest source of engagement. Audiences grow quickly on Facebook but can disappear even more quickly; in the case of left-leaning pages, many had accumulated followings not just by speaking to Sanders supporters but also by being intensely critical, and often utterly dismissive, of Clinton.

Now that the nomination contest is over, Rivero has turned to making anti-Trump content. A post from earlier this month got straight to the point: "Donald Trump is unqualified, unstable and unfit to lead. Share if you agree!" More than 40,000 people did.

"It's like a meme war," Rivero says, "and politics is being won and lost on social media."

In retrospect, Facebook's takeover of online media looks rather like a slow-motion coup. Before social media, web publishers could draw an audience one of two ways: through a dedicated readership visiting its home page or through search engines. By 2009, this had started to change. Facebook had more than 300 million users, primarily accessing the service through desktop browsers, and publishers soon learned that a widely shared link could produce substantial traffic. In 2010, Facebook released widgets that publishers could embed on their sites, reminding readers to share, and these tools were widely deployed. By late 2012, when Facebook passed a billion users, referrals from the social network were sending visitors to publishers' websites at rates sometimes comparable to Google, the web's previous de facto distribution hub. Publishers took note of what worked on Facebook and adjusted accordingly.

This was, for most news organizations, a boon. The flood of visitors aligned with two core goals of most media companies: to reach people and to make money. But as Facebook's growth continued, its influence was intensified by broader trends in internet use, primarily the use of smartphones, on which Facebook became more deeply enmeshed with users' daily routines. Soon, it became clear that Facebook wasn't just a source of readership; it was, increasingly, where readers lived.

Facebook, from a publisher's perspective, had seized the web's means of distribution by popular demand. A new reality set in, as a social-media network became an intermediary between publishers and their audiences. For media companies, the ability to reach an audience is fundamentally altered, made greater in some ways and in others more challenging. For a dedicated Facebook user, a vast array of sources, spanning multiple media and industries, is now processed through the same interface and sorting mechanism, alongside updates from friends, family, brands and celebrities.

From the start, some publishers cautiously regarded Facebook as a resource to be used only to the extent that it supported their existing businesses, wary of giving away more than they might get back. Others embraced it more fully, entering into formal partnerships for revenue sharing and video production, as The New York Times has done. Some new-media start-ups, most notably BuzzFeed, have pursued a comprehensively Facebook-centric production-and-distribution strategy. All have eventually run up against the same reality: A company that can claim nearly every internet-using adult as a user is less a partner than a context — a self-contained marketplace to which you have been granted access but which functions according to rules and incentives that you cannot control.

The news feed is designed, in Facebook's public messaging, to "show people the stories most relevant to them" and ranks stories "so that what's most important to each person shows up highest in their news feeds." It is a framework built around personal connections and sharing, where value is both expressed and conferred through the concept of engagement. Of course, engagement, in one form or another, is what media businesses have always sought, and provocation has always sold news. But now the incentives are literalized in buttons and written into software.

Any sufficiently complex system will generate a wide variety of results, some expected, some not; some desired, others less so. On July 31, a Facebook page called Make America Great posted its final story of the day. "No Media Is Telling You About the Muslim Who Attacked Donald Trump, So We Will ...," read the headline, next to a small avatar of a pointing and yelling Trump. The story was accompanied by a photo of Khizr Khan, the father of a slain American soldier. Khan spoke a few days earlier at the Democratic National Convention, delivering a searing speech admonishing Trump for his comments about Muslims. Khan, pocket Constitution in hand, was juxtaposed with the logo of the Muslim Brotherhood in Egypt. "It is a sad day in America," the caption read, "where we the people must expose the TRUTH because the media is in the tank for 1 Presidential Candidate!"

Readers who clicked through to the story were led to an external website, called Make America Great Today, where they were presented with a brief write-up blended almost seamlessly into a solid wall of fleshy ads. Khan, the story said — between ads for "(1) Odd Trick to 'Kill' Herpes Virus for Good" and "22 Tank Tops That Aren't Covering Anything" — is an agent of the Muslim Brotherhood and a "promoter of Islamic Shariah law." His late son, the story suggests, could have been a "Muslim martyr" working as a double agent. A credit link beneath the story led to a similar-looking site called Conservative Post, from which the story's text was pulled verbatim. Conservative Post had apparently sourced its story from a longer post on a right-wing site called Shoebat.com.

Within 24 hours, the post was shared more than 3,500 times, collecting a further 3,000 reactions — thumbs-up likes, frowning emoji, angry emoji — as well as 850 comments, many lengthy and virtually all impassioned. A modest success. Each day, according to Facebook's analytics, posts from the Make America Great page are seen by 600,000 to 1.7 million people. In July, articles posted to the page, which has about 450,000 followers, were shared, commented on or liked more than four million times, edging out, for example, the Facebook page of USA Today.

Make America Great, which inhabits the fuzzy margins of the political Facebook page ecosystem, is owned and operated by a 35-year-old online marketer named Adam Nicoloff. He started the page in August 2015 and runs it from his home outside St. Louis. Previously, Nicoloff provided web services and marketing help for local businesses; before that, he worked in restaurants. Today he has shifted his focus to Facebook pages and websites that he administers himself. Make America Great was his first foray into political pages, and it quickly became the most successful in a portfolio that includes men's lifestyle and parenting.

Nicoloff's business model is not dissimilar from the way most publishers use Facebook: build a big following, post links to articles on an outside website covered in ads and then hope the math works out in your favor. For many, it doesn't: Content is expensive, traffic is unpredictable and website ads are both cheap and alienating to readers. But as with most of these Facebook-native pages, Nicoloff's content costs comparatively little, and the sheer level of interest in Trump and in the type of inflammatory populist rhetoric he embraces has helped tip Nicoloff's system of advertising arbitrage into serious profitability. In July, visitors arriving to Nicoloff's website produced a little more than $30,000 in revenue. His costs, he said, total around $8,000, partly split between website hosting fees and advertising buys on Facebook itself.

Then, of course, there's the content, which, at a few dozen posts a day, Nicoloff is far too busy to produce himself. "I have two people in the Philippines who post for me," Nicoloff said, "a husband-and-wife combo." From 9 a.m. Eastern time to midnight, the contractors scour the internet for viral political stories, many explicitly pro-Trump. If something seems to be going viral elsewhere, it is copied to their site and promoted with an urgent headline. (The Khan story was posted at the end of the shift, near midnight Eastern time, or just before noon in Manila.) The resulting product is raw and frequently jarring, even by the standards of this campaign. "There's No Way I'll Send My Kids to Public School to Be Brainwashed by the LGBT Lobby," read one headline, linking to an essay ripped from Glenn Beck's The Blaze; "Alert:

UN Backs Secret Obama Takeover of Police; Here's What We Know ...,"
read another, copied from a site called The Federalist Papers Project. In the end, Nicoloff takes home what he jokingly described as a "doctor's salary" — in a good month, more than $20,000.

Terry Littlepage, an internet marketer based in Las Cruces, N.M., has taken this model even further. He runs a collection of about 50 politically themed Facebook pages with names like The American Patriot and My Favorite Gun, which push visitors to a half-dozen external websites, stocked with content aggregated by a team of freelancers. He estimates that he spends about a thousand dollars a day advertising his pages on Facebook; as a result, they have more than 10 million followers. In a good month, Littlepage's properties bring in $60,000.

Nicoloff and Littlepage say that Trump has been good for business, but each admits to some discomfort. Nicoloff, a conservative, says that there were other candidates he preferred during the Republican primaries but that he had come around to the nominee. Littlepage is also a recent convert. During the primaries, he was a Cruz supporter, and he even tried making some left-wing pages on Facebook but discovered that they just didn't make him as much money.

In their angry, cascading comment threads, Make America Great's followers express no such ambivalence. Nearly every page operator I spoke to was astonished by the tone their commenters took, comparing them to things like torch-wielding mobs and sharks in a feeding frenzy. No doubt because of the page's name, some Trump supporters even mistake Nicoloff's page for an official organ of the campaign. Nicoloff says that he receives dozens of messages a day from Trump supporters, expecting or hoping to reach the man himself. Many, he says, are simply asking for money.

Many of these political news pages will likely find their cachet begin to evaporate after Nov. 8. But one company, the Liberty Alliance, may have found a way to create something sustainable and even potentially transformational, almost entirely within the ecosystem of Facebook. The Georgia-based firm was founded by Brandon Vallorani, formerly of Answers in Genesis, the organization that opened a museum in Kentucky promoting a literal biblical creation narrative. Today the Liberty Alliance has around 100 sites in its network, and about 150 Facebook pages, according to Onan Coca, the company's 36-year-old editor in chief. He estimates their cumulative follower count to be at least 50 million. Among the company's partners are the former congressman Allen West, the 2008 election personality Joe the Plumber, the conservative actor Kirk Cameron and the former "Saturday Night Live" cast member Victoria Jackson. Then there are Liberty's countless news-oriented pages, which together have become an almost ubiquitous presence on right-leaning political Facebook in the last few years. Their names are instructive and evocative: Eagle Rising; Fighting for Trump; Patriot Tribune; Revive America; US Herald; The Last Resistance.

A dozen or so of the sites are published in-house, but posts from the company's small team of writers are free to be shared among the entire network. The deal for a would-be Liberty Alliance member is this: You bring the name and the audience, and the company will build you a prefab site, furnish it with ads, help you fill it with content and keep a cut of the revenue. Coca told me the company brought in $12 million in revenue last year. (The company declined to share documentation further corroborating his claims about followers and revenue.)

Because the pages are run independently, the editorial product is varied. But it is almost universally tuned to the cadences and styles that seem to work best on partisan Facebook. It also tracks closely to conservative Facebook media's big narratives, which, in turn, track with the Trump campaign's messaging: Hillary Clinton is a crook and possibly mentally unfit; ISIS is winning; Black Lives Matter is the real racist movement; Donald Trump alone can save us; the system — all of it — is rigged. Whether the Liberty Alliance succeeds or fails will depend, at least in part, on Facebook's algorithm. Systemic changes to the ecosystem arrive through algorithmic adjustments, and the company recently adjusted the news feed to "further reduce clickbait headlines."

For now, the network hums along, mostly beneath the surface. A post from a Liberty Alliance page might find its way in front of a left-leaning user who might disagree with it or find it offensive, and who might choose to engage with the friend who posted it directly. But otherwise, such news exists primarily within the feeds of the already converted, its authorship obscured, its provenance unclear, its veracity questionable. It's an environment that's at best indifferent and at worst hostile to traditional media brands; but for this new breed of page operator, it's mostly upside. In front of largely hidden and utterly sympathetic audiences, incredible narratives can take shape, before emerging, mostly formed, into the national discourse.

Consider the trajectory of a post from August, from a Facebook page called Patriotic Folks, the headline of which read, "Spread This: Media Rigging the Polls, Hiding New Evidence Proving Trump Is Winning." The article cited a litany of social-media statistics highlighting Trump's superior engagement numbers, among them Trump's Facebook following, which is nearly twice as large as Clinton's. "Don't listen to the lying media — the only legitimate attack they have left is Trump's poll numbers," it said. "Social media proves the GOP nominee has strong foundation and a firm backing." The story spread across this right-wing Facebook ecosystem, eventually finding its way to Breitbart and finally to Sean Hannity's "Morning Minute," where he read through the statistics to his audience.

Before Hannity signed off, he posed a question: "So, does that mean anything?" It's a version of the question that everyone wants to answer about Facebook and politics, which is whether the site's churning political warfare is actually changing minds — or, for that matter, beginning to change the political discourse as a whole. How much of what happens on the platform is a reflection of a political mood and widely held beliefs, simply captured in a new medium, and how much of it might be created, or intensified, by the environment it provides? What is Facebook doing to our politics?

Appropriately, the answer to this question can be chosen and shared on Facebook in whichever way you prefer. You might share this story from The New York Times Magazine, wondering aloud to your friends whether our democracy has been fundamentally altered by this publishing-and-advertising platform of unprecedented scale. Or you might just relax and find some memes to share from one of countless pages that will let you air your political id. But for the page operators, the question is irrelevant to the task at hand. Facebook's primacy is a foregone conclusion, and the question of Facebook's relationship to political discourse is absurd — they're one and the same. As Rafael Rivero put it to me, "Facebook is where it's all happening."

JOHN HERRMAN is a David Carr fellow at The New York Times.

Facebook and the Digital Virus Called Fake News

EDITORIAL | BY THE NEW YORK TIMES | NOV. 19, 2016

THIS YEAR, THE ADAGE that "falsehood flies and the truth comes limping after it" doesn't begin to describe the problem. That idea assumes that the truth eventually catches up. There's not much evidence of this happening for the millions of people taken in by the fake news stories — like Pope Francis endorsing Donald Trump or Mr. Trump pulling ahead of Hillary Clinton in the popular vote — that have spread on social media sites.

Most of the fake news stories are produced by scammers looking to make a quick buck. The vast majority of them take far-right positions. But a big part of the responsibility for this scourge rests with internet companies like Facebook and Google, which have made it possible for fake news to be shared nearly instantly with millions of users and have been slow to block it from their sites.

Mark Zuckerberg, the founder and chief executive of Facebook, has dismissed the notion that fake news is prevalent on his platform or that it had an influence on the election. But according to a Buzz-Feed News analysis, during the last three months of the presidential campaign, the 20 top fake news stories on Facebook generated more engagement — shares, likes and comments — than the 20 top stories from real news websites.

These hoaxes are not just bouncing around among like-minded conspiracy theorists; candidates and elected officials are sharing them, too. Senator Ben Sasse, Republican of Nebraska, on Thursday tweeted about people who have been paid to riot against Mr. Trump — an idea propagated by fake news stories. A man who wrote a number of false news reports told The Washington Post that Trump support-ers and campaign officials often shared his false anti-Clinton posts without bothering to confirm the facts and that he believes his work may have helped elect the Republican nominee.

Abroad, the dissemination of fake news on Facebook, which reaches 1.8 billion people globally, has been a longstanding problem. In countries like Myanmar, deceptive internet content has reportedly contributed to ethnic violence. And it has influenced elections in Indonesia, the Philippines and elsewhere. Social media sites have also been used to spread misinformation about the referendum on the peace deal in Colombia and about Ebola in West Africa.

Facebook says it is working on weeding out such fabrications. It said last Monday that it would no longer place Facebook-powered ads on fake news websites, a move that could cost Facebook and those fake news sites a lucrative source of revenue. Earlier on the same day, Google said it would stop letting those sites use its ad placement network. These steps would help, but Facebook, in particular, owes its users, and democracy itself, far more.

Facebook has demonstrated that it can effectively block content like click-bait articles and spam from its platform by tweaking its algorithms, which determine what links, photos and ads users see in their news feeds. Nobody outside the company knows exactly how its software works and why you might see posts shared by some of your friends frequently and others rarely. Recently, the company acknowledged that it had allowed businesses to target or exclude users for ads for housing, employment and credit based on their ethnicity, in apparent violation of anti-discrimination laws. It has said it will stop that practice.

Facebook managers are constantly changing and refining the algorithms, which means the system is malleable and subject to human judgment. This summer, Facebook decided to show more posts from friends and family members in users' news feeds and reduce stories from news organizations, because that's what it said users wanted. If it can do that, surely its programmers can train the software to spot bogus stories and outwit the people producing this garbage.

Blocking misinformation will help protect the company's brand and credibility. Some platforms have suffered when they have failed to address users' concerns. Twitter users, for instance, have backed away from that platform because of abusive trolling, threatening posts and hate speech, which the company hasn't been able to control.

Mr. Zuckerberg himself has spoken at length about how social media can help improve society. In a 2012 letter to investors, he said it could "bring a more honest and transparent dialogue around government that could lead to more direct empowerment of people, more accountability for officials and better solutions to some of the biggest problems of our time."

None of that will happen if he continues to let liars and con artists hijack his platform.

Facebook's Problem Isn't Fake News — It's the Rest of the Internet

BY JOHN HERRMAN | DEC. 22, 2016

LAST THURSDAY, AFTER WEEKS of criticism over its role in the prolifera-tion of falsehoods and propaganda during the presidential election, Facebook announced its plan to combat "hoaxes" and "fake news." The company promised to test new tools that would allow users to report misinformation, and to enlist fact-checking organizations including Snopes and PolitiFact to help litigate the veracity of links reported as suspect. By analyzing patterns of reading and shar-ing, the company said, it might be able to penalize articles that are shared at especially low rates by those who read them — a signal of dissatisfaction. Finally, it said, it would try to put economic pressure on bad actors in three ways: by banning disputed stories from its advertising ecosystem; by making it harder to impersonate credible sites on the platform; and, crucially, by penalizing websites that are loaded with too many ads.

Over the past month the colloquial definition of "fake news" has expanded beyond usefulness, implicating everything from partisan news to satire to conspiracy theories before being turned, finally, back against its creators. Facebook's fixes address a far more narrow defi-nition. "We've focused our efforts on the worst of the worst, on the clear hoaxes spread by spammers for their own gain," wrote Adam Mosseri, a vice president for news feed, in a blog post.

Facebook's political news ecosystem during the 2016 election was vast and varied. There was, of course, content created by outside news media that was shared by users, but there were also reams of content — posts, images, videos — created on Facebook-only pages, and still more media created by politicians themselves. During the election, it was apparent to almost anyone with an account that Facebook was teeming with political content, much of it extremely partisan or pitched, its sourcing sometimes obvious, other times obscured, and often simply beside the point — memes or rants or theories that spoke for themselves.

Facebook seems to have zeroed in on only one component of this ecosystem — outside websites — and within it, narrow types of bad actors. These firms are, generally speaking, paid by advertising companies independent of Facebook, which are unaware of or indifferent to their partners' sources of audience. Accordingly, Facebook's anti-hoax measures seek to regulate these sites by punishing them not just for what they do on Facebook, but for what they do outside of it.

"We've found that a lot of fake news is financially motivated," Mosseri wrote. "Spammers make money by masquerading as well-known news organizations and posting hoaxes that get people to visit to their sites, which are often mostly ads." The proposed solution: "Analyzing publisher sites to detect where policy enforcement actions might be necessary."

The stated targets of Facebook's efforts are precisely defined, but its formulation of the problem implicates, to a lesser degree, much more than just "the worst of the worst." Consider this characterization of what makes a "fake news" site a bad platform citizen: It uses Facebook to capture receptive audiences by spreading lies and then converts those audiences into money by borrowing them from Facebook, luring them to an outside site larded with obnoxious ads. The site's sin of fabrication is made worse by its profit motive, which is cast here as a sort of arbitrage scheme. But an acceptable news site does more or less the same thing: It uses Facebook to capture receptive audiences by spreading not-lies and then converts those audiences into money by luring them to an outside site not-quite larded with not-as-obnoxious ads. In either case, Facebook users are being taken out of the safe confines of the platform into areas that Facebook does not and cannot control.

In this context, this "fake news" problem reads less as a distinct new phenomenon than as a flaring symptom of an older, more existential anxiety that Facebook has been grappling with for years: its continued (albeit diminishing) dependence on the same outside web that it, and other platforms, have begun to replace. Facebook's plan for "fake news" is no doubt intended to curb certain types of misinformation. But it's also a continuation of the company's bigger and more consequential project — to capture the experiences of the web it wants and from which it can profit, but to insulate itself from the parts that it doesn't and can't. This may help solve a problem within the ecosystem of outside publishers — an ecosystem that, in the distribution machinery of Facebook, is becoming redundant, and perhaps even obsolete.

As Facebook has grown, so have its ambitions. Its mantralike mission (to "connect the world") is rivaled among internet companies perhaps by only that of Google (to "organize the world's information") in terms of sheer scope. In the run-up to Facebook's initial public offering, Mark Zuckerberg told investors that the company makes decisions "not optimizing for what's going to happen in the next year, but to set us up to really be in this world where every product experience you have is social, and that's all powered by Facebook."

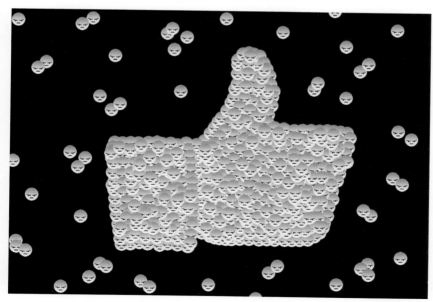

ALVARO DOMINGUEZ

To understand what such ambition looks like in practice, consider Facebook's history. It started as an inward-facing website, closed off from both the web around it and the general public. It was a place to connect with other people, and where content was created primarily by other users: photos, wall posts, messages. This system quickly grew larger and more complex, leading to the creation, in 2006, of the news feed — a single location in which users could find updates from all of their Facebook friends, in roughly reverse-chronological order.

When the news feed was announced, before the emergence of the modern Facebook sharing ecosystem, Facebook's operating definition of "news" was pointedly friend-centric. "Now, whenever you log in, you'll get the latest headlines generated by the activity of your friends and social groups," the announcement about the news feed said. This would soon change.

In the ensuing years, as more people spent more time on Facebook, and following the addition of "Like" and "Share" functions within Facebook, the news feed grew into a personalized portal not just for personal updates but also for the cornucopia of media that existed elsewhere online: links to videos, blog posts, games and more or less anything else published on an external website, including news articles. This potent mixture accelerated Facebook's change from a place for keeping up with family and friends to a place for keeping up, additionally, with the web in general, as curated by your friends and family. Facebook's purview continued to widen as its user base grew and then acquired their first smartphones; its app became an essential lens through which hundreds of millions of people interacted with one another, with the rest of the web and, increasingly, with the world at large.

Facebook, in other words, had become an interface for the whole web rather than just one more citizen of it. By sorting and mediating the internet, Facebook inevitably began to change it. In the previous decade, the popularity of Google influenced how websites worked, in noticeable ways: Titles and headlines were written in search-friendly formats; pages or articles would be published not just to cover the news but, more specifically, to address Google searchers' queries *about* the news, the canonical example being The Huffington Post's famous "What Time Does The Super Bowl Start?" Publishers built entire business models around attracting search traffic, and search-engine optimization, S.E.O., became an industry unto itself. Facebook's influence on the web — and in particular, on news publishers — was similarly profound. Publishers began taking into consideration how their headlines, and stories, might travel within Facebook. Some embraced the site as a primary source of visitors; some pursued this strategy into absurdity and exploitation.

Facebook, for its part, paid close attention to the sorts of external content people were sharing on its platform and to the techniques used by websites to get an edge. It adapted continually. It provided greater video functionality, reducing the need to link to outside videos or embed them from YouTube. As people began posting more news, it created previews for links, with larger images and headlines and longer summaries; eventually, it created Instant Articles, allowing certain publishers (including The Times) to publish stories natively in Facebook. At the same time, it routinely sought to penalize sites it judged to be using the platform in bad faith, taking aim at "clickbait," an older cousin of "fake news," with a series of design and algorithm updates. As Facebook's influence over online media became unavoidably obvious, its broad approach to users and the web became clearer: If the network became a popular venue for a certain sort of content or behavior, the company generally and reasonably tried to make that behavior easier or that content more accessible. This tended to mean, however, bringing it in-house.

To Facebook, the problem with "fake news" is not just the obvious damage to the discourse, but also with the harm it inflicts upon the platform. People sharing hoax stories were, presumably, happy enough with what they were seeing. But the people who would then encounter those stories in their feeds were subjected to a less positive experience. They were sent outside the platform to a website where they realized they were being deceived, or where they were exposed to ads or something that felt like spam, or where they were persuaded to share something that might later make them look like a rube. These users might rightly associate these experiences not just with their friends on the platform, or with the sites peddling the bogus stories but also with the platform itself. This created, finally, an obvious issue for a company built on attention, advertising and the promotion of outside brands. From the platform's perspective, "fake news" is essentially a user-experience problem resulting from a lingering design issue — akin to slow-loading news websites that feature auto-playing videos and obtrusive ads.

Increasingly, legitimacy within Facebook's ecosystem is conferred according to a participant's relationship to the platform's design. A verified user telling a lie, be it a friend from high school or the president elect, isn't breaking the rules; he is, as his checkmark suggests, who he represents himself to be. A post making false claims about a product is Facebook's problem only if that post is labeled an ad. A user video promoting a conspiracy theory becomes a problem only when it leads to the violation of community guidelines against, for example, user harassment. Facebook contains a lot more than just news, including a great deal of content that is newslike, partisan, widely shared and often misleading. Content that has been, and will be, immune from current "fake news" critiques and crackdowns, because it never had the opportunity to declare itself news in the first place. To publish lies as "news" is to break a promise; to publish lies as "content" is not.

That the "fake news" problem and its proposed solutions have been defined by Facebook as link issues — as a web issue — aligns nicely with a longer-term future in which Facebook's interface with the web is diminished. Indeed, it heralds the coming moment when posts from outside are suspect by default: out of place, inefficient, little better than spam.

JOHN HERRMAN is a David Carr fellow at The New York Times.

How Climate Change Deniers Rise to the Top in Google Searches

BY HIROKO TABUCHI | DEC. 29, 2017

TYPE THE WORDS "climate change" into Google and you could get an unexpected result: advertisements that call global warming a hoax.

"Scientists blast climate alarm," said one that appeared at the top of the search results page during a recent search, pointing to a website, DefyCCC, that asserted: "Nothing has been studied better and found more harmless than anthropogenic CO_2 release."

Another ad proclaimed: "The Global Warming Hoax — Why the Science Isn't Settled," linking to a video containing unsupported assertions, including that there is no correlation between rising levels of greenhouse gases and higher global temperatures.

(In reality, the harmful effects of carbon dioxide emissions linked to human activity, like rising temperatures and melting sea ice, have been acknowledged by every major scientific organization in the world.)

America's technology giants have come under fire for their role in the spread of fake news during the 2016 presidential campaign, prompting promises from Google and others to crack down on sites that spread disinformation.

Less scrutinized has been the way tech companies continue to provide a mass platform for the most extreme sites among those that use false or misleading science to reject the overwhelming scientific consensus on climate change. Google's search page has become an especially contentious battleground between those who seek to educate the public on the established climate science and those who reject it.

Not everyone who uses Google will see climate denial ads in their search results. Google's algorithms use search history and other data to tailor ads to the individual, something that is helping to create a highly partisan internet.

A recent search for "climate change" or "global warming" from a Google account linked to a New York Times climate reporter did not return any denial ads. The top results were ads from environmental groups like the Natural Resources Defense Council and the Environmental Defense Fund.

But when the same reporter searched for those terms using private browsing mode, which helps mask identity information from Google's algorithms, the ad for DefyCCC popped up.

"These are the info wars," said Robert J. Brulle, a Drexel University professor of sociology and environmental science who has studied climate advocacy and misinformation. "It's becoming harder and harder for the individual to find unbiased information that they can trust, because there's so much other material trying to crowd that space."

After being contacted by The New York Times in mid-December, Google said it had removed an ad from its climate search results, though it declined to identify which one. An ad from DefyCCC was still turning up at the top of searches days later. As of Wednesday, no ads at all were turning up for Times reporters and editors running these searches.

The climate denialist ads are an example of how contrarian groups can use the internet's largest automated advertising systems to their advantage, gaming the system to find a mass platform for false or misleading claims.

Google allows companies to bid on search terms, and displays paid content at the top of its search results in the same blue font used for unpaid content. (For example, a candy maker might bid on the term "Christmas candy" so that its ads pop up when someone searches for those words.) Google identifies ads in its search results with an icon below the link.

"We have extensive policies that protect users, advertisers and publishers from harmful, misleading, and deceptive content," a Google spokeswoman, Elisa Greene, said in a statement. She said that last year the company had removed 1.7 billion ads and 100,000 publishers for policy violations in its ad network.

Google's AdWords policy on misrepresentation states that it does not want users "to feel misled by ads that we deliver, so we strive to be clear and honest, and provide the information that users need to make informed decisions." But that policy focuses on consumer protection — for example, guarding against concealed subscription or shipping costs — not on the veracity of other content.

Many media organizations have come under fire for giving a platform to climate change denialists in the interest of balance, and policies on paid advertisements vary.

A spokeswoman for The New York Times, Danielle Rhoades Ha, said that the paper's advertising acceptability standards prohibited obvious falsehoods, so it would not accept an ad that said climate change is not happening or that human beings have played no role in it. Steve Severinghaus, a spokesman for The Wall Street Journal, said the paper accepted "a wide range of advertisements, including those with provocative viewpoints."

The climate denial ads on Google come amid a wider effort — backed by wealthy conservatives, fossil fuel companies and right-wing think tanks — to discredit the prevailing science on global warming and to prevent action.

DefyCCC, the site that recently bought the "climate change" search term on Google, devotes an entire section of its site to content from WattsUpWithThat, a well-known climate denial site by the blogger Anthony Watts. Mr. Watts has received funding from the Heartland Institute, backed by the billionaire Koch brothers.

Beyond that, little is known about DefyCCC. Its domain was registered through DomainsByProxy, a service that allows owners to keep their personal information secret.

Reached by phone in Austin, Tex., Leo Goldstein, DefyCCC's founder, said he had started the site in 2015, and that CCC stood for "climate change cult — which sounds like an exaggeration, but it's not."

He said he aimed to combat what he saw as alarmism over science that he argued was not settled. He received help with his site but would not say who his backers were to protect their privacy. "I can tell you it's not the fossil fuel industry," he said.

He said that advertising on Google had dramatically increased his site's visitor numbers. Traffic to DefyCCC has surged almost 2,000 percent over the past six months, with much of the increase since late September, according to data from web analytics firm SimilarWeb.

"Of course, people click," said Mr. Goldstein, who said he had emigrated from Russia two decades ago and had worked in the software and power industries. "Google is the No. 1 advertising choice."

The proliferation of climate disinformation, both online and off, has coincided with an effort to undermine measures to combat climate change. Republican leaders regularly question climate science and President Trump has called climate change a hoax. He announced plans to withdraw from the global Paris accord on climate change and is aggressively rolling back environmental regulations.

Fewer than a third of registered Republicans nationwide say that climate change is caused mostly by human activities, according to a new study published in the journal Climatic Change by researchers at the University of California Santa Barbara, Yale University and Utah State University.

The Natural Resources Defense Council buys Google search terms as "a tool we use to help connect with people who want to get informed and get involved in the fight against climate change," said Margie Kelly, a spokeswoman for the environmental group. The Environmental Defense Fund did not respond to requests for comment.

Jeffrey Harvey, a population ecologist at the Netherlands Institute of Ecology, recently published a study on blogs that deny the well-documented impacts of climate change and Arctic ice loss on polar bears. He said that contrarian ads on web search results, which many users considered to be neutral territory, were especially problematic.

"If you search for 'global warming' and 'polar bear,' you'll often get bombarded with sites that are ignoring the scientific evidence," he said. "I think this is something that search engines need to address."

CHAPTER 6

Tech Companies Under Scrutiny

After several years of scandal, digital platforms are attracting more robust criticism for their inner workings. Though
tech companies have begun making changes, larger struc-
tural problems of consumer privacy may lead to government action. Mark Zuckerberg, founder of Facebook, has
attempted to foster a public dialogue about improving the
platform, while skeptical voices suggest that social media's
problems cannot be solved without stricter regulation.

Can Facebook Fix Its Own Worst Bug?

BY FARHAD MANJOO | APRIL 25, 2017

Mark Zuckerberg now acknowledges the dangerous side of the social revolution
he helped start. But is the most powerful tool for connection in human history
capable of adapting to the world it created?

IN EARLY JANUARY, I went to see Mark Zuckerberg at MPK20, a
concrete-and-steel building on the campus of Facebook's headquarters, which sits across a desolate highway from the marshy salt flats
of Menlo Park, Calif. The Frank Gehry-designed building has a pris-
tine nine-acre rooftop garden, yet much of the interior — a mean-
dering open-plan hallway — appears unfinished. There are exposed
air ducts and I-beams scribbled with contractors' marks. Many of
the internal walls are unpainted plywood. The space looks less like
the headquarters of one of the world's wealthiest companies and

more like a Chipotle with standing desks. It's an aesthetic meant to reflect — and perhaps also inspire employee allegiance to — one of Facebook's founding ideologies: that things are never quite finished, that nothing is permanent, that you should always look for a chance to take an ax to your surroundings.

The mood in overwhelmingly liberal Silicon Valley at the time, days before Donald Trump's inauguration, was grim. But Zuckerberg, who had recently returned from his 700-acre estate on the Hawaiian island of Kauai, is preternaturally unable to look anything other than excited about the future. "Hey, guys!" he beamed, greeting me and Mike Isaac, a Times colleague who covers Facebook. Zuckerberg wore a short-sleeve gray T-shirt, jeans and sneakers, which is his Steve Jobsian daily uniform: Indoor Zuck.

Zuckerberg used to be a nervous speaker, but he has become much less so. He speaks quickly but often unloads full paragraphs of thought, and sometimes his arguments are so polished that they sound rehearsed, which happened often that morning. "2016 was an interesting year for us," he said as the three of us, plus a P.R. executive, sat around a couple of couches in the glass-walled conference room where he conducts many of his meetings. (There are many perks to working at Facebook, but no one, not even Zuckerberg, has a private office.) It was an understatement and a nod to the obvious: Facebook, once a mere app on your phone, had become a global political and cultural force, and the full implications of that transformation had begun to come into view last year. "If you look at the history of Facebook, when we started off, there really wasn't news as part of it," Zuckerberg went on. But as Facebook grew and became a bigger part of how people learn about the world, the company had been slow to adjust to its new place in people's lives. The events of 2016, he said, "set off a number of conversations that we're still in the middle of."

Nearly two billion people use Facebook every month, about 1.2 billion of them daily. The company, which Zuckerberg co-founded in his Harvard dorm room 13 years ago, has become the largest and most influential entity in the news business, commanding an audience greater than that of any American or European television news network, any newspaper or magazine in the Western world and any online news outlet. It is also the most powerful mobilizing force in politics, and it is fast replacing television as the most consequential entertainment medium. Just five years after its initial public offering, Facebook is one of the 10 highest market-capitalized public companies in the world.

As recently as a year ago, Zuckerberg might have proudly rattled off these facts as a testament to Facebook's power. But over the course of 2016, Facebook's gargantuan influence became its biggest liability. During the U.S. election, propagandists — some working for money, others for potentially state-sponsored lulz — used the service to turn fake stories into viral sensations, like the one about Pope Francis' endorsing Trump (he hadn't). And fake news was only part of a larger conundrum. With its huge reach, Facebook has begun to act as the great disseminator of the larger cloud of misinformation and half-truths swirling about the rest of media. It sucks up lies from cable news and Twitter, then precisely targets each lie to the partisan bubble most receptive to it.

After studying how people shared 1.25 million stories during the campaign, a team of researchers at M.I.T. and Harvard implicated Facebook and Twitter in the larger failure of media in 2016. The researchers found that social media created a right-wing echo chamber: a "media network anchored around Breitbart developed as a distinct and insulated media system, using social media as a backbone to transmit a hyperpartisan perspective to the world." The findings partially echoed a long-held worry about social news: that people would use sites like Facebook to cocoon themselves into self-reinforcing bubbles of confirmatory ideas, to the detriment of civility and a shared factual basis from which to make collective, democratic decisions. A week and a half after the election, President Obama bemoaned "an age where there's so much active misinformation and it's packaged very well and it looks the same when you see it on a Facebook page or you turn on your television."

After the election, Zuckerberg offered a few pat defenses of Facebook's role. "I'm actually quite proud of the impact that we were able to have on civic discourse over all," he said when we spoke in January. Misinformation on Facebook was not as big a problem as some believed it was, but Facebook nevertheless would do more to battle it, he pledged. Echo chambers were a concern, but if the source was people's own confirmation bias, was it really Facebook's problem to solve?

It was hard to tell how seriously Zuckerberg took the criticisms of his service and its increasingly paradoxical role in the world. He had spent much of his life building a magnificent machine to bring people together. By the most literal measures, he'd succeeded spectacularly, but what had that connection wrought? Across the globe, Facebook now seems to benefit actors who want to undermine the global vision at its foundation. Supporters of Trump and the European right-wing nationalists who aim to turn their nations inward and dissolve alliances, trolls sowing cross-border paranoia, even ISIS with its skillful social-media recruiting and propagandizing — all of them have sought in their own ways to split the Zuckerbergian world apart. And they are using his own machine to do it.

In Silicon Valley, current events tend to fade into the background. The Sept. 11 attacks, the Iraq war, the financial crisis and every recent presidential election occurred, for the tech industry, on some parallel but distant timeline divorced from the everyday business of digitizing the world. Then Donald Trump won. In the 17 years I've spent covering Silicon Valley, I've never seen anything shake the place like his victory. In the span of a few months, the Valley has been transformed from a politically disengaged company town into a center of anti-Trump resistance and fear. A week after the election, one start-up founder sent me a private message on Twitter: "I think it's worse than I thought," he wrote. "Originally I thought 18 months. I've cut that in half." Until what? "Apocalypse. End of the world."

Trump's campaign rhetoric felt particularly personal for an industry with a proud reliance upon immigrants. Stephen K. Bannon, Trump's campaign chief executive and now chief White House strategist, once suggested that there were too many South Asian chief executives in tech. More than 15 percent of Facebook's employees are in the United States on H-1B visas, a program that Trump has pledged to revamp. But the outcome also revealed the depth of the Valley's disconnection with much of the rest of the country. "I saw an election that was just different from the way I think," says Joshua Reeves, a Bay Area native who is a co-founder of Gusto, a human-resources software start-up. "I have this engineering brain that wants to go to this analytical, rational, nonemotional way of looking at things, and it was clear in this election that we're trending in a different direction, toward spirited populism."

Underneath it all was a nagging feeling of complicity. Trump had benefited from a media environment that is now shaped by Facebook — and, more to the point, shaped by a single Facebook feature, the same one to which the company owes its remarkable ascent to social-media hegemony: the computationally determined list of updates you see every time you open the app. The list has a formal name, News Feed. But most users are apt to think of it as Facebook itself.

If it's an exaggeration to say that News Feed has become the most influential source of information in the history of civilization, it is only slightly so. Facebook created News Feed in 2006 to solve a problem: In the social-media age, people suddenly had too many friends to keep up with. At the time, Facebook was just a collection of profiles, lacking any kind of central organization. To figure out what any of your connections were up to, you had to visit each of their profiles to see if anything had changed. News Feed fixed that. Every time you open Facebook, it hunts through the network, collecting every post from every connection — information that, for most Facebook users, would be too overwhelming to process themselves. Then it weighs the merits of each post before presenting you with a feed sorted in order of importance: a hyperpersonalized front page designed just for you.

Scholars and critics have been warning of the solipsistic irresistibility of algorithmic news at least since 2001, when the constitutional-law professor Cass R. Sunstein warned, in his book "Republic.com," of the urgent risks posed to democracy "by any situation in which thousands or perhaps millions or even tens of millions of people are mainly listening to louder echoes of their own voices." (In 2008, I piled on with my own book, "True Enough: Learning to Live in a Post-Fact Society.") In 2011, the digital activist and entrepreneur Eli Pariser, looking at similar issues, gave this phenomenon a memorable name in the title of his own book: "The Filter Bubble."

Facebook says its own researchers have been studying the filter bubble since 2010. In 2015, they published an in-house study, which was criticized by independent researchers, concluding that Facebook's effect on the diversity of people's information diet was minimal. News Feed's personalization algorithm did filter out some opposing views in your feed, the study claimed, but the bigger effect was users' own choices. When News Feed did show people views contrary to their own, they tended not to click on the stories. For Zuckerberg, the finding let Facebook off the hook. "It's a good-sounding theory, and I can get why people repeat it, but it's not true," he said on a call with analysts last summer.

Employees got the same message. "When Facebook cares about something, they spin up teams to address it, and Zuck will come out and talk about it all the time," one former executive told me. "I have never heard of anything close to that on the filter bubble. I never sensed that this was a problem he wanted us to tackle. It was always positioned as an interesting intellectual question but not something that we're going to go focus on."

Then, last year, Facebook's domination of the news became a story itself. In May, Gizmodo reported that some editors who had worked on Facebook's Trending Topics section had been suppressing conservative points of view. To smooth things over, Zuckerberg convened a meeting of conservative media figures and eventually significantly reduced the role of human editors. Then in September, Facebook deleted a post by a Norwegian writer that included the photojournalist Nick Ut's iconic photo of a naked 9-year-old girl, Phan Thi Kim Phuc, running in terror after a napalm attack during the Vietnam War, on the grounds that it ran afoul of Facebook's prohibition of child nudity.

Facebook, under criticism, reinstated the picture, but the photo incident stuck with Zuckerberg. He would bring it up unbidden to staff members and to reporters. It highlighted, for him, the difficulty of building a policy framework for what Facebook was trying to do. Zuckerberg wanted to become a global news distributor that is run by machines, rather than by humans who would try to look at every last bit of content and exercise considered judgment. "It's something I think we're still figuring out," he told me in January. "There's a lot more to do here than what we've done. And I think we're starting to realize this now as well."

It struck me as an unsatisfying answer, and it later became apparent that Zuckerberg seemed to feel the same way. On a Sunday morning about a month after the first meeting, I got a call from a Facebook spokesman. Zuckerberg wanted to chat again. Could Mike and I come back on Monday afternoon?

We met again in the same conference room. Same Zuck outfit, same P.R. executive. But the Zuckerberg who greeted us seemed markedly different. He was less certain in his pronouncements than he had been the month before, more expansive and questioning. Earlier that day, Zuckerberg's staff had sent me a draft of a 5,700-word manifesto that, I was told, he spent weeks writing. The document, "Building Global Community," argued that until now, Facebook's corporate goal had merely been to connect people. But that was just Step 1. According to the manifesto, Facebook's "next focus will be developing the social infrastructure for community — for supporting us, for keeping us safe, for informing us, for civic engagement, and for inclusion of all." If it was a nebulous crusade, it was also vast in its ambition.

The last manifesto that Zuckerberg wrote was in 2012, as part of Facebook's application to sell its stock to the public. It explained Facebook's philosophy — what he called "the hacker way" — and sketched an unorthodox path for the soon-to-be-public company. "Facebook was not originally created to be a company," he wrote. "It was built to accomplish a social mission: to make the world more open and connected."

What's striking about that 2012 letter, read through the prism of 2017, is its certainty that a more "open and connected" world is by definition a better one. "When I started Facebook, the idea of connecting the world was not controversial," Zuckerberg said now. "The default assumption was that the world was incrementally just moving in that direction. So I thought we can connect some people and do our part in helping move in that direction." But now, he said, whether it was wise to connect the world was "actually a real question."

Zuckerberg's new manifesto never quite accepts blame for any of the global ills that have been laid at Facebook's feet. Yet by the standards of a company release, it is remarkable for the way it concedes that the company's chief goal — wiring the globe — is controversial. "There are questions about whether we can make a global community that works for everyone," Zuckerberg writes, "and whether the path ahead is to connect more or reverse course." He also confesses misgivings about Facebook's role in the news. "Giving everyone a voice has historically been a very positive force for public discourse because it increases the diversity of ideas shared," he writes. "But the past year has also shown it may fragment our shared sense of reality."

At the time of our second interview, the manifesto was still only a draft, and I was surprised by how unsure Zuckerberg seemed about it in person. He had almost as many questions for us — about whether we understood what he was trying to say, how we thought it would land in the media — as we had for him. When I suggested that it might be perceived as an attack on Trump, he looked dismayed. He noted several times that he had been noodling over these ideas since long before November. A few weeks earlier, there was media speculation, fueled by a postelection tour of America by Zuckerberg and his wife, that he was laying the groundwork to run against Trump in 2020, and in this meeting he took pains to shoot down the rumors. When I asked if he had chatted with Obama about the former president's critique of

Facebook, Zuckerberg paused for several seconds, nearly to the point of awkwardness, before answering that he had.

Facebook's spokespeople later called to stress that Obama was only one of many people to whom he had spoken. In other words: Don't read this as a partisan anti-Trump manifesto. But if the company pursues the admittedly airy aims outlined in "Building Global Community," the changes will echo across media and politics, and some are bound to be considered partisan. The risks are especially clear for changes aimed at adding layers of journalistic ethics across News Feed, which could transform the public's perception of Facebook, not to mention shake the foundations of its business.

The Facebook app, and consequently News Feed, is run by one of Zuckerberg's most influential lieutenants, a 34-year-old named Chris Cox, the company's chief product officer. Ten years ago, Cox dropped out of a graduate program in computer science at Stanford to join Facebook. One of his first assignments was on the team that created News Feed. Since then, he has become an envoy to the media industry. Don Graham, the longtime publisher of The Washington Post who was for years a member of Facebook's board, told me that he felt Cox, among Facebook staff, "was at the 99.9th percentile of interest in news. He thought it was important to society, and he wanted Facebook to get it right."

For the typical user, Cox explained when I met him on a morning in October at MPK20, News Feed is computing the relative merits of about 2,000 potential posts in your network every time you open the app. In sorting these posts, Facebook does not optimize for any single metric: not clicks or reading time or likes. Instead, he said, "what you really want to get to is whether somebody, at the end of the day, would say, 'Hey, my experience today was meaningful.' " Personalizing News Feed, in other words, is a very big "math problem," incorporating countless metrics in extraordinarily complicated ways. Zuckerberg calls it "a modern A.I. problem."

Last summer, I sat in on two meetings in another glass-walled MPK20 conference room, in which News Feed's engineers, designers, user-research experts and managers debated several small alterations to how News Feed displays certain kinds of posts. The conversations were far from exciting — people in jeans on couches looking at PowerPoints, talking quietly about numbers — and yet I found them mesmerizing, a demonstration of the profound cultural differences between how news companies like The Times work and how Facebook does. The first surprise was how slowly things move, contrary to the freewheeling culture of "the hacker way." In one meeting, the team spent several minutes discussing the merits of bold text in a certain News Feed design. One blessing of making social software is that you can gauge any potential change to your product by seeing how your users react to it. That is also the curse: At Facebook, virtually every change to the app, no matter how small or obviously beneficial, is thoroughly tested on different segments of the audience before it's rolled out to everyone.

The people who work on News Feed aren't making decisions that turn on fuzzy human ideas like ethics, judgment, intuition or seniority. They are concerned only with quantifiable outcomes about people's actions on the site. That data, at Facebook, is the only real truth. And it is a particular kind of truth: The News Feed team's ultimate mission is to figure out what users want — what they find "meaningful," to use Cox and Zuckerberg's preferred term — and to give them more of that.

This ideal runs so deep that the people who make News Feed often have to put aside their own notions of what's best. "One of the things we've all learned over the years is that our intuition can be wrong a fair amount of the time," John Hegeman, the vice president of product management and a News Feed team member, told me. "There are things you don't expect will happen. And we learn a lot from that process: Why didn't that happen, and what might that mean?" But it is precisely this ideal that conflicts with attempts to wrangle the feed in the way press critics have called for. The whole purpose of editorial guidelines and ethics is often to suppress individual instincts in favor of some larger social goal. Facebook finds it very hard to suppress anything that its users' actions say they want. In some cases, it has been easier for the company to seek out evidence that, in fact, users don't want these things at all.

Facebook's two-year-long battle against "clickbait" is a telling example. Early this decade, the internet's headline writers discovered the power of stories that trick you into clicking on them, like those that teasingly withhold information from their headlines: "Dustin Hoffman Breaks Down Crying Explaining Something That Every Woman Sadly Already Experienced." By the fall of 2013, clickbait had overrun News Feed. Upworthy, a progressive activism site co-founded by Pariser, the author of "The Filter Bubble," that relied heavily on teasing headlines, was attracting 90 million readers a month to its feel-good viral posts.

If a human editor ran News Feed, she would look at the clickbait scourge and make simple, intuitive fixes: Turn down the Upworthy knob. But Facebook approaches the feed as an engineering project rather than an editorial one. When it makes alterations in the code that powers News Feed, it's often only because it has found some clear signal in its data that users are demanding the change. In this sense, clickbait was a riddle. In surveys, people kept telling Facebook that they hated teasing headlines. But if that was true, why were they clicking on them? Was there something Facebook's algorithm was missing, some signal that would show that despite the clicks, clickbait was really sickening users?

To answer these questions, Cox and his team hired survey panels of more than a thousand paid "professional raters" around the world who answer questions about how well News Feed is working. Starting in 2013, Facebook began adding first dozens and then hundreds and then thousands of data points that were meant to teach the artificial-intelligence system that runs News Feed how people were reacting to their feeds. Facebook noticed that people would sometimes click open a clickbaity story but spend very little time on it. In other cases, lots of people would click on a story but few would share or Like it. Headlines on stories that people seemed to reject often contained a set of signature phrases ("you'll never believe," "this one trick," etc.) or they came from a set of repeat-offender publishers.

The more such signals Facebook incorporated into the feed, the more clickbait began to drop out of the feed. Since its 2013 peak, Upworthy's traffic has declined; it now averages 17.5 million visitors a month. The site has since disavowed clickbait. "We sort of unleashed a monster," Peter Koechley, Upworthy's co-founder, told a conference in 2015. "Sorry for that."

Cox suggested that it was not exactly correct to say that Facebook, as a company, decided to fight clickbait. What actually happened was that Facebook found better ways to listen to users, who were themselves rejecting clickbait. "That comes out of good-quality panels and measurement systems, rather than an individual decision saying, 'Hey, I really want us to care about clickbait,' " he says.

This approach — looking for signs of user dissatisfaction — could curb stories that constitute the most egregious examples of misinformation. Adam Mosseri, Facebook's vice president in charge of News Feed, says that Facebook has begun testing an algorithm change that would look at whether people share an article after reading it. If few of the people who click on a story decide to share it, that might suggest people feel misled by it and it would get lower billing in the feed.

But the solution to the broader misinformation dilemma — the pervasive climate of rumor, propaganda and conspiracy theories that Facebook has inadvertently incubated — may require something that Facebook has never done: ignoring the likes and dislikes of its users. Facebook believes the pope-endorses-Trump type of made-up news stories are only a tiny minority of pieces that appear in News Feed; they account for a fraction of 1 percent of the posts, according to Mosseri. The question the company faces now is whether the misinformation problem resembles clickbait at all, and whether its solutions will align as neatly with Facebook's worldview. Facebook's entire project, when it comes to news, rests on the assumption that people's individual preferences ultimately coincide with the public good, and that if it doesn't appear that way at first, you're not delving deeply enough into the data. By contrast, decades of social-science research shows that most of us simply prefer stuff that feels true to our worldview even if it isn't true at all and that the mining of all those preference signals is likely to lead us deeper into bubbles rather than out of them.

After the election, Margaret Sullivan, the Washington Post columnist and a former public editor of The Times, called on Facebook to hire an executive editor who would monitor News Feed with an eye to fact-checking, balance and editorial integrity. Jonah Peretti, the founder of BuzzFeed, told me that he wanted Facebook to use its data to create a kind of reputational score for online news, as well as explore ways of strengthening reporting through monetary partnerships.

"At some point, if they really want to address this, they have to say, 'This is good information' and 'This is bad information,'" says Emily Bell, the director for the Tow Center for Digital Journalism at Columbia Journalism School. "They have to say, 'These are the kinds of information sources that we want to privilege, and these others are not going to be banned from the platform, but they are not going to thrive.' In other words, they have to create a hierarchy, and they're going to have to decide how they're going to transfer wealth into the publishing market."

There aren't many technical reasons Facebook could not implement such plans. The hurdles are institutional and philosophical, and ultimately financial too. Late last year, Facebook outlined a modest effort to curb misinformation. News Feed would now carry warning labels: If a friend shares a viral story that has been flagged and shot down by one of Facebook's fact-checking partners (including Snopes and PolitiFact), you'll be cautioned that the piece has been "disputed." But even that slight change has been met with fury on the right, with Breitbart and The Daily Caller fuming that Facebook had teamed up with liberal hacks motivated by partisanship. If Facebook were to take more significant action, like hiring human editors, creating a reputational system or paying journalists, the company would instantly become something it has long resisted: a media company rather than a neutral tech platform.

In many ways, the worry over how Facebook changes the news is really a manifestation of a grander problem with News Feed, which is simply dominance itself. News Feed's aggressive personalization wouldn't be much of an issue if it weren't crowding out every other source. "To some degree I feel like the Pottery Barn Rule applies," says Pariser, the Upworthy chief executive. "They play a critical role in our information circulatory system, and so — lucky them — all of the problems therein are significantly on their shoulders."

During our first meeting in January, I posed this question to Zuckerberg: "When you see various problems in the media, do you say to yourself, 'I run Facebook, I can solve that?'"

"Um," he started, and then paused, weighing his words as carefully as American presidents once did. "Not usually." He argued that some of Facebook's critics' proposed fixes for news on the service, such as hiring editors, were impractical due to Facebook's scale and global diversity. Personalization, he said, remained a central tenet. "It really gets back to, like, what do people want at a deep level," he said. "There's this oversimplified narrative that a company can get very successful by just scratching a very superficial itch, and I don't really think that's right over the long term."

Yet by our second meeting, Zuckerberg's position seemed to have evolved. Facebook had by then announced plans for the Facebook Journalism Project, in which the company would collaborate with news companies on new products. Facebook also created a project to promote "news literacy" among its users, and it hired the former CNN news anchor Campbell Brown to manage the partnership between it and news companies. Zuckerberg's tone toward critics of Facebook's approach to news had also grown far more conciliatory. "I think it's really important to get to the core of the actual problem," he said. "I also really think that the core social thing that needs to happen is that a common understanding needs to exist. And misinformation I view as one of the things that can possibly erode common understanding. But sensationalism and polarization and other things, I actually think, are probably even stronger and more prolific effects. And we have to work on all these things. I think we need to listen to all the feedback on this."

Still, in both our conversation and his new manifesto, Zuckerberg remained preoccupied with the kind of problems that could be solved by the kind of hyperconnectivity he believed in, not the ones caused by it. "There's a social infrastructure that needs to get built for modern problems in order for humanity to get to the next level," he said. "Having more people oriented not just toward short-term things but toward building the long-term social infrastructure that needs to get built across all these things in order to enable people to come together is going to be a really important thing over the next decades." By way of example, he pointed to Safety Check, Facebook's system for letting people tell their friends that they've survived some kind of dangerous event, like a natural disaster or terrorist attack.

"We're getting to a point where the biggest opportunities I think in the world … problems like preventing pandemics from spreading or ending terrorism, all these things, they require a level of coordination and connection that I don't think can only be solved by the current systems that we have," Zuckerberg told me. What's needed, he argues, is some global superstructure to advance humanity.

This is not an especially controversial idea; Zuckerberg is arguing for a kind of digital-era version of the global institution-building that the Western world engaged in after World War II. But because he is a chief executive and not an elected president, there is something frightening about his project. He is positioning Facebook — and, considering that he commands absolute voting control of the company, he is positioning himself — as a critical enabler of the next generation of human society. A minor problem with his mission is that it drips with megalomania, albeit of a particularly sincere sort. With his wife, Priscilla

Chan, Zuckerberg has pledged to give away nearly all of his wealth to a variety of charitable causes, including a long-term medical-research project to cure all disease. His desire to take on global social problems through digital connectivity, and specifically through Facebook, feels like part of the same impulse.

Yet Zuckerberg is often blasé about the messiness of the transition between the world we're in and the one he wants to create through software. Building new "social infrastructure" usually involves tearing older infrastructure down. If you manage the demolition poorly, you might undermine what comes next. In the case of the shattering media landscape, Zuckerberg seems finally to have at least noticed this problem and may yet come up with fixes for it. But in the meantime, Facebook rushes headlong into murky new areas, uncovering new dystopian possibilities at every turn.

A few months after I spoke with Zuckerberg, Facebook held its annual developer conference in San Jose, Calif. At last year's show, Zuckerberg introduced an expanded version of Facebook's live streaming service which had been promised to revolutionize how we communicate. In the year since, Live had generated iconic scenes of protest, but it was also used to broadcast a terrorist attack in Munich and at least one suicide. Hours before Zuckerberg's appearance at the conference, police announced that a Cleveland man who had killed a stranger and posted a video on Facebook had shot himself after a manhunt.

But as he took the stage in San Jose, Zuckerberg was ebullient. He started with a few dad jokes and threatened to read his long manifesto on stage. For a brief moment, there was a shift in tone: Statesman Zuck. "In all seriousness, this is an important time to work on building community," he said. He offered Facebook's condolences to the victim in Cleveland; the incident, he said, reminded Facebook that "we have a lot more to do."

Just as quickly, though, Zuckerberg then pivoted to Facebook's next marvel, a system for digitally augmenting your pictures and videos. The technical term for this is "augmented reality." The name bursts with dystopian possibilities — fake news on video rather than just text — but Zuckerberg never mentioned them. The statesman had left the stage; before us stood an engineer.

FARHAD MANJOO is a technology columnist for The New York Times. He is working on a book about what he calls the Frightful Five: Apple, Amazon, Google, Facebook and Microsoft — the five technology giants that are swallowing up the rest of the economy.

Just Don't Call It Privacy

ANALYSIS | BY NATASHA SINGER | SEPT. 22, 2018

Amazon, Google and Twitter executives are heading to Congress. Should legislators give consumers control over the data companies have on them?

WHAT DO YOU CALL IT when employers use Facebook's advertising platform to show certain job ads only to men or just to people between the ages of 25 and 36?

How about when Google collects the whereabouts of its users — even after they deliberately turn off location history?

Or when AT&T shares its mobile customers' locations with data brokers?

American policymakers often refer to such issues using a default umbrella term: privacy. That at least is the framework for a Senate Commerce Committee hearing scheduled for this Wednesday titled "Examining Safeguards for Consumer Data Privacy."

After a spate of recent data-mining scandals — including Russian-sponsored ads on Facebook aimed at influencing African-Americans not to vote — some members of Congress are now rallying behind the idea of a new federal consumer privacy law.

At this week's hearing, legislators plan to ask executives from Amazon, AT&T, Google, Twitter and other companies about their privacy policies. Senators also want the companies to explain "what Congress can do to promote clear privacy expectations without hurting innovation," according to the hearing notice.

There's just one flaw with this setup.

In a surveillance economy where companies track, analyze and capitalize on our clicks, the issue at hand isn't privacy. The problem is unfettered data exploitation and its potential deleterious consequences — among them, unequal consumer treatment, financial fraud, identity theft, manipulative marketing and discrimination.

In other words, asking companies whose business models revolve around exploiting data-based consumer-influence techniques to explain their privacy policies seems about as useful as asking sharks to hold forth on veganism.

"Congress should not be examining privacy policies," Marc Rotenberg, the executive director of the Electronic Privacy Information Center, a prominent digital rights nonprofit, told me last week. "They should be examining business practices. They should be examining how these firms collect and use the personal data of customers, of internet users."

The Senate Commerce hearing, however, doesn't seem designed to investigate commercial surveillance and influence practices that might merit government oversight.

For one thing, only industry executives are currently set to testify. And most of them are lawyers and policy experts, not engineers versed in the mechanics of data-mining algorithms.

Companies are sending their "policy and law folks to Washington to make the government go away — not the engineering folks who actually understand these systems in depth and can talk through alternatives," Jonathan Mayer, an assistant professor of computer science and public affairs at Princeton University, told me.

That may be because Congress is under industry pressure.

California recently passed a new privacy law that would give Californians some power over the data companies' hold on them. Industry groups hope to defang that statute by pushing Congress to pass federal privacy legislation that would overrule state laws. The industry-stacked Senate hearing lineup seems designed to pave the way for that, said Danielle Citron, a law professor at the University of Maryland.

Frederick Hill, a spokesman for the Senate Commerce Committee, said the group planned future hearings that would include other voices, such as consumer groups. But "for the first hearing," Mr. Hill said, "the committee is bringing in companies most consumers recognize to make the discussion about privacy more relatable."

What is at stake here isn't privacy, the right not to be observed. It's how companies can use our data to invisibly shunt us in directions that may benefit them more than us.

Many consumers know that digital services and ad tech companies track and analyze their activities. And they accept, or are at least resigned to, data-mining in exchange for conveniences like customized newsfeeds and ads.

But revelations about Russian election interference and Cambridge Analytica, the voter-profiling company that obtained information on millions of Facebook users, have made it clear that data-driven influence campaigns can scale quickly and cause societal harm.

And that leads to a larger question: Do we want a future in which companies can freely parse the photos we posted last year, or the location data from the fitness apps we used last week, to infer whether we are stressed or depressed or financially strapped or emotionally vulnerable — and take advantage of that?

"Say I sound sick when I am talking to Alexa, maybe they would show me medicine as a suggestion on Amazon," said Franziska

Roesner, an assistant professor of computer science at the University of Washington, using a hypothetical example of Amazon's voice assistant. "What happens when the inferences are wrong?"

(Amazon said it does not use Alexa data for product recommendations or marketing.)

It's tough to answer those questions right now when there are often gulfs between the innocuous ways companies explain their data practices to consumers and the details they divulge about their targeting techniques to advertisers.

AT&T's privacy policy says the mobile phone and cable TV provider may use third-party data to categorize subscribers, without using their real names, into interest segments and show them ads accordingly. That sounds reasonable enough.

Here's what it means in practice: AT&T can find out which subscribers have indigestion — or at least which ones bought over-the-counter drugs to treat it.

In a case study for advertisers, AT&T describes segmenting DirecTV subscribers who bought antacids and then targeting them with ads for the medication. The firm was also able to track those subscribers' spending. Households who saw the antacid ads spent 725 percent more on the drugs than a national audience.

Michael Balmoris, a spokesman for AT&T, said the company's privacy policy was "transparent and precise, and describes in plain language how we use information and the choices we give customers."

But consumer advocates hope senators will press AT&T, Amazon and other companies this week to provide more details on their consumer-profiling practices. "We want an inside look on the analytics and how they're categorizing, ranking, rating and scoring us," Professor Citron said.

Given the increased public scrutiny, some companies are tweaking their tactics.

AT&T recently said it would stop sharing users' location details with data brokers. Facebook said it had stopped allowing advertisers to use sensitive categories, like race or religion, to exclude people from seeing ads. Google created a feature for users to download masses of their data, including a list of all the sites Google has tracked them on.

Government officials in Europe are not waiting for companies to police themselves. In May, the European Union introduced a tough new data protection law that curbs some data-mining.

It requires companies to obtain explicit permission from European users before collecting personal details on sensitive subjects like their religion, health or sex life. It gives European users the right to see all of the information companies hold about them — including any algorithmic scores or inferences.

European users also have the right not to be subject to completely automated decisions that could significantly affect them, such as credit algorithms that use a person's data to decide whether a bank should grant him or her a loan.

Of course, privacy still matters. But Congress now has an opportunity to press companies like Amazon on broader public issues. It could require them to disclose exactly how they use data extracted from consumers. And it could force companies to give consumers some rights over that data.

NATASHA SINGER is a business reporter covering health technology, education technology and consumer privacy.

As Facebook Raised a Privacy Wall, It Carved an Opening for Tech Giants

BY GABRIEL J.X. DANCE, MICHAEL LAFORGIA AND NICHOLAS CONFESSORE | DEC. 18, 2018

Internal documents show that the social network gave Microsoft, Amazon, Spotify and others far greater access to people's data than it has disclosed.

FOR YEARS, FACEBOOK gave some of the world's largest technology companies more intrusive access to users' personal data than it has disclosed, effectively exempting those business partners from its usual privacy rules, according to internal records and interviews.

The special arrangements are detailed in hundreds of pages of Facebook documents obtained by The New York Times. The records, generated in 2017 by the company's internal system for tracking partnerships, provide the most complete picture yet of the social network's data-sharing practices. They also underscore how personal data has become the most prized commodity of the digital age, traded on a vast scale by some of the most powerful companies in Silicon Valley and beyond.

The exchange was intended to benefit everyone. Pushing for explosive growth, Facebook got more users, lifting its advertising revenue. Partner companies acquired features to make their products more attractive. Facebook users connected with friends across different devices and websites. But Facebook also assumed extraordinary power over the personal information of its 2.2 billion users — control it has wielded with little transparency or outside oversight.

Facebook allowed Microsoft's Bing search engine to see the names of virtually all Facebook users' friends without consent, the records show, and gave Netflix and Spotify the ability to read Facebook users' private messages.

The social network permitted Amazon to obtain users' names and contact information through their friends, and it let Yahoo view streams of friends' posts as recently as this summer, despite public statements that it had stopped that type of sharing years earlier.

Facebook has been reeling from a series of privacy scandals, set off by revelations in March that a political consulting firm, Cambridge Analytica, improperly used Facebook data to build tools that aided President Trump's 2016 campaign. Acknowledging that it had breached users' trust, Facebook insisted that it had instituted stricter privacy protections long ago. Mark Zuckerberg, the chief executive, assured lawmakers in April that people "have complete control" over everything they share on Facebook.

But the documents, as well as interviews with about 50 former employees of Facebook and its corporate partners, reveal that Facebook allowed certain companies access to data despite those protections. They also raise questions about whether Facebook ran afoul of a 2011 consent agreement with the Federal Trade Commission that barred the social network from sharing user data without explicit permission.

In all, the deals described in the documents benefited more than 150 companies — most of them tech businesses, including online retailers and entertainment sites, but also automakers and media organizations. Their applications sought the data of hundreds of millions of people a month, the records show. The deals, the oldest of which date to 2010, were all active in 2017. Some were still in effect this year.

In an interview, Steve Satterfield, Facebook's director of privacy and public policy, said none of the partnerships violated users' privacy or the F.T.C. agreement. Contracts required the companies to abide by Facebook policies, he added.

Still, Facebook executives have acknowledged missteps over the past year. "We know we've got work to do to regain people's trust," Mr. Satterfield said. "Protecting people's information requires stronger teams, better technology and clearer policies, and that's where we've been focused for most of 2018." He said that the partnerships were "one area of focus" and that Facebook was in the process of winding many of them down.

Facebook has found no evidence of abuse by its partners, a spokeswoman said. Some of the largest partners, including Amazon, Microsoft and Yahoo, said they had used the data appropriately, but declined to discuss the sharing deals in detail. Facebook did say that it had mismanaged some of its partnerships, allowing certain companies' access to continue long after they had shut down the features that required the data.

With most of the partnerships, Mr. Satterfield said, the F.T.C. agreement did not require the social network to secure users' consent before sharing data because Facebook considered the partners extensions of itself — service providers that allowed users to interact with their Facebook friends. The partners were prohibited from using the personal information for other purposes, he said. "Facebook's partners don't get to ignore people's privacy settings."

Data privacy experts disputed Facebook's assertion that most partnerships were exempted from the regulatory requirements, expressing skepticism that businesses as varied as device makers, retailers and search companies would be viewed alike by the agency. "The only common theme is that they are partnerships that would benefit the company in terms of development or growth into an area that they otherwise could not get access to," said Ashkan Soltani, former chief technologist at the F.T.C.

Mr. Soltani and three former employees of the F.T.C.'s consumer protection division, which brought the case that led to the consent decree, said in interviews that its data-sharing deals had probably violated the agreement.

"This is just giving third parties permission to harvest data without you being informed of it or giving consent to it," said David Vladeck, who formerly ran the F.T.C.'s consumer protection bureau. "I don't understand how this unconsented-to data harvesting can at all be justified under the consent decree."

Details of the agreements are emerging at a pivotal moment for the world's largest social network. Facebook has been hammered with questions about its data sharing from lawmakers and regulators in the United States and Europe. The F.T.C. this spring opened a new inquiry into Facebook's compliance with the consent order, while the Justice Department and Securities and Exchange Commission are also investigating the company.

Facebook's stock price has fallen, and a group of shareholders has called for Mr. Zuckerberg to step aside as chairman. Shareholders also have filed a lawsuit alleging that executives failed to impose effective privacy safeguards. Angry users started a #DeleteFacebook movement.

This month, a British parliamentary committee investigating internet disinformation released internal Facebook emails, seized from the plaintiff in another lawsuit against Facebook. The messages disclosed some partnerships and depicted a company preoccupied with growth, whose leaders sought to undermine competitors and briefly considered selling access to user data.

As Facebook has battled one crisis after another, the company's critics, including some former advisers and employees, have singled out the data-sharing as cause for concern.

"I don't believe it is legitimate to enter into data-sharing partnerships where there is not prior informed consent from the user," said Roger McNamee, an early investor in Facebook. "No one should trust Facebook until they change their business model."

AN ENGINE FOR GROWTH

Personal data is the oil of the 21st century, a resource worth billions to those who can most effectively extract and refine it. American companies alone are expected to spend close to $20 billion by the end of 2018 to acquire and process consumer data, according to the Interactive Advertising Bureau.

Few companies have better data than Facebook and its rival, Google, whose popular products give them an intimate view into the daily lives of billions of people — and allow them to dominate the digital advertising market.

Facebook has never sold its user data, fearful of user backlash and wary of handing would-be competitors a way to duplicate its most prized asset. Instead, internal documents show, it did the next best thing: granting other companies access to parts of the social network in ways that advanced its own interests.

Facebook began forming data partnerships when it was still a relatively young company. Mr. Zuckerberg was determined to weave Facebook's services into other sites and platforms, believing it would stave off obsolescence and insulate Facebook from competition. Every corporate partner that integrated Facebook data into its online products helped drive the platform's expansion, bringing in new users, spurring them to spend more time on Facebook and driving up advertising revenue. At the same time, Facebook got critical data back from its partners.

The partnerships were so important that decisions about forming them were vetted at high levels, sometimes by Mr. Zuckerberg and Sheryl Sandberg, the chief operating officer, Facebook officials said. While many of the partnerships were announced publicly, the details of the sharing arrangements typically were confidential.

Sheryl Sandberg, Facebook's second-in-command, at a Senate hearing in September. The data-sharing deals were vetted at senior levels, sometimes by her and Mr. Zuckerberg, Facebook officials said.

By 2013, Facebook had entered into more such partnerships than its midlevel employees could easily track, according to interviews with two former employees. (Like the more than 30 other former employees interviewed for this article, they spoke on the condition of anonymity because they had signed nondisclosure agreements or still maintained relationships with top Facebook officials.)

So they built a tool that did the technical work of turning special access on and off and also kept records on what are known internally as "capabilities" — the special privileges enabling companies to obtain data, in some cases without asking permission.

The Times reviewed more than 270 pages of reports generated by the system — records that reflect just a portion of Facebook's wide-ranging deals. Among the revelations was that Facebook obtained data from multiple partners for a controversial friend-suggestion tool called "People You May Know."

The feature, introduced in 2008, continues even though some Facebook users have objected to it, unsettled by its knowledge of their real-world relationships. Gizmodo and other news outlets have reported cases of the tool's recommending friend connections between patients of the same psychiatrist, estranged family members, and a harasser and his victim.

Facebook, in turn, used contact lists from the partners, including Amazon, Yahoo and the Chinese company Huawei — which has been flagged as a security threat by American intelligence officials — to gain deeper insight into people's relationships and suggest more connections, the records show.

Some of the access deals described in the documents were limited to sharing non-identifying information with research firms or enabling game makers to accommodate huge numbers of players. These raised no privacy concerns. But agreements with about a dozen companies did. Some enabled partners to see users' contact information through their friends — even after the social network, responding to complaints, said in 2014 that it was stripping all applications of that power.

As of 2017, Sony, Microsoft, Amazon and others could obtain users' email addresses through their friends.

Facebook also allowed Spotify, Netflix and the Royal Bank of Canada to read, write and delete users' private messages, and to see all participants on a thread — privileges that appeared to go beyond what the companies needed to integrate Facebook into their systems, the records show. Facebook acknowledged that it did not consider any of those three companies to be service providers. Spokespeople for Spotify and Netflix said those companies were unaware of the broad powers Facebook had granted them. A spokesman for Netflix said Wednesday that it had used the access only to enable customers to recommend TV shows and movies to their friends.

"Beyond these recommendations, we never accessed anyone's personal messages and would never do that," he said.

A Royal Bank of Canada spokesman disputed that the bank had had any such access. (Aspects of some sharing partnerships, including those with the Royal Bank of Canada and Bing, were first reported by The Wall Street Journal.)

Spotify, which could view messages of more than 70 million users a month, still offers the option to share music through Facebook Messenger. But Netflix and the Canadian bank no longer needed access to messages because they had deactivated features that incorporated it.

These were not the only companies that had special access longer than they needed it. Yahoo, The Times and others could still get Facebook users' personal information in 2017.

Yahoo could view real-time feeds of friends' posts for a feature that the company had ended in 2012. A Yahoo spokesman declined to discuss the partnership in detail but said the company did not use the information for advertising. The Times — one of nine media companies named in the documents — had access to users' friend lists for an article-sharing application it had discontinued in 2011. A spokeswoman for the news organization said it was not obtaining any data.

Facebook's internal records also revealed more about the extent of sharing deals with over 60 makers of smartphones, tablets and other devices, agreements first reported by The Times in June.

Facebook empowered Apple to hide from Facebook users all indicators that its devices were asking for data. Apple devices also had access to the contact numbers and calendar entries of people who had changed their account settings to disable all sharing, the records show.

Apple officials said they were not aware that Facebook had granted its devices any special access. They added that any shared data remained on the devices and was not available to anyone other than the users.

Facebook officials said the company had disclosed its sharing deals in its privacy policy since 2010. But the language in the policy about its service providers does not specify what data Facebook shares, and with which companies. Mr. Satterfield, Facebook's privacy director, also said its partners were subject to "rigorous controls."

Yet Facebook has an imperfect track record of policing what outside companies do with its user data. In the Cambridge Analytica case, a Cambridge University psychology professor created an application in 2014 to harvest the personal data of tens of millions of Facebook users for the consulting firm.

Pam Dixon, executive director of the World Privacy Forum, a nonprofit privacy research group, said that Facebook would have little power over what happens to users' information after sharing it broadly. "It travels," Ms. Dixon said. "It could be customized. It could be fed into an algorithm and decisions could be made about you based on that data."

400 MILLION EXPOSED

Unlike Europe, where social media companies have had to adapt to stricter regulation, the United States has no general consumer privacy law, leaving tech companies free to monetize most kinds of personal information as long as they don't mislead their users. The F.T.C., which regulates trade, can bring enforcement actions against companies that deceive their customers.

Besides Facebook, the F.T.C. has consent agreements with Google and Twitter stemming from alleged privacy violations.

Facebook's agreement with regulators is a result of the company's early experiments with data sharing. In late 2009, it changed the privacy settings of the 400 million people then using the service, making some of their information accessible to all of the internet. Then it shared that information, including users' locations and religious and political leanings, with Microsoft and other partners.

Facebook called this "instant personalization" and promoted it as a step toward a better internet, where other companies would use the information to customize what people saw on sites like Bing. But the feature drew complaints from privacy advocates and many Facebook users that the social network had shared the information without permission.

The F.T.C. investigated and in 2011 cited the privacy changes as a deceptive practice. Caught off guard, Facebook officials stopped mentioning instant personalization in public and entered into the consent agreement.

Under the decree, the social network introduced a "comprehensive privacy program" charged with reviewing new products and features. It was initially overseen by two chief privacy officers, their lofty title an apparent sign of Facebook's commitment. The company also hired PricewaterhouseCoopers to assess its privacy practices every two years.

But the privacy program faced some internal resistance from the start, according to four former Facebook employees with direct knowledge of the company's efforts. Some engineers and executives, they said, considered the privacy reviews an impediment to quick innovation and growth. And the core team responsible for coordinating the reviews — numbering about a dozen people by 2016 — was moved around within Facebook's sprawling organization, sending mixed signals about how seriously the company took it, the ex-employees said.

Critically, many of Facebook's special sharing partnerships were not subject to extensive privacy program reviews, two of the former employees said. Executives believed that because the partnerships were governed by business contracts requiring them to follow Facebook data policies, they did not require the same level of scrutiny. The privacy team had limited ability to review or suggest changes to some of those data-sharing agreements, which had been negotiated by more senior officials at the company.

Facebook officials said that members of the privacy team had been consulted on the sharing agreements, but that the level of review "depended on the specific partnership and the time it was created."

In 2014, Facebook ended instant personalization and walled off access to friends' information. But in a previously unreported agreement, the social network's engineers continued allowing Bing; Pandora, the music streaming service; and Rotten Tomatoes, the movie and television review site, access to much of the data they had gotten for the discontinued feature. Bing had access to the information through last year, the records show, and the two other companies did as of late summer, according to tests by The Times.

Facebook officials said the data sharing did not violate users' privacy because it allowed access only to public data — though that included data that the social network had made public in 2009. They added that the social network made a mistake in allowing the access to continue for the three companies, but declined to elaborate. Spokeswomen for Pandora and Rotten Tomatoes said the businesses were not aware of any special access.

Facebook also declined to discuss the other capabilities Bing was given, including the ability to see all users' friends.

Microsoft officials said that Bing was using the data to build profiles of Facebook users on Microsoft servers. They declined to provide details, other than to say the information was used in "feature development" and not for advertising. Microsoft has since deleted the data, the officials said.

COMPLIANCE QUESTIONS

For some advocates, the torrent of user data flowing out of Facebook has called into question not only Facebook's compliance with the F.T.C. agreement, but also the agency's approach to privacy regulation.

"There has been an endless barrage of how Facebook has ignored users' privacy settings, and we truly believed that in 2011 we had solved this problem," said Marc Rotenberg, head of the Electronic Privacy Information Center, an online privacy group that filed one of the first complaints about Facebook with federal regulators. "We brought Facebook under the regulatory authority of the F.T.C. after a tremendous amount of work. The F.T.C. has failed to act."

According to Facebook, most of its data partnerships fall under an exemption to the F.T.C. agreement. The company argues that the partner companies are service providers — companies that use the data only "for and at the direction of" Facebook and function as an extension of the social network.

But Mr. Vladeck and other former F.T.C. officials said that Facebook was interpreting the exemption too broadly. They said the provision was intended to allow Facebook to perform the same everyday functions as other companies, such as sending and receiving information over the internet or processing credit card transactions, without violating the consent decree.

When The Times reported last summer on the partnerships with device makers, Facebook used the term "integration partners" to describe BlackBerry, Huawei and other manufacturers that pulled Facebook data to provide social-media-style features on smartphones. All such integration partners, Facebook asserted, were covered by the service provider exemption.

Since then, as the social network has disclosed its data sharing deals with other kinds of businesses — including internet companies such as Yahoo — Facebook has labeled them integration partners, too.

Facebook even recategorized one company, the Russian search giant Yandex, as an integration partner.

Facebook records show Yandex had access in 2017 to Facebook's unique user IDs even after the social network stopped sharing them with other applications, citing privacy risks. A spokeswoman for Yandex, which was accused last year by Ukraine's security service of funneling its user data to the Kremlin, said the company was unaware of the access and did not know why Facebook had allowed it to continue. She added that the Ukrainian allegations "have no merit."

In October, Facebook said Yandex was not an integration partner. But in early December, as The Times was preparing to publish this article, Facebook told congressional lawmakers that it was.

An F.T.C. spokeswoman declined to comment on whether the commission agreed with Facebook's interpretation of the service provider exception, which is likely to figure in the F.T.C.'s ongoing Facebook investigation. She also declined to say whether the commission had ever received a complete list of partners that Facebook considered service providers.

But federal regulators had reason to know about the partnerships — and to question whether Facebook was adequately safeguarding users' privacy. According to a letter that Facebook sent this fall to Senator Ron Wyden, the Oregon Democrat, PricewaterhouseCoopers reviewed at least some of Facebook's data partnerships.

The first assessment, sent to the F.T.C. in 2013, found only "limited" evidence that Facebook had monitored those partners' use of data. The finding was redacted from a public copy of the assessment, which gave Facebook's privacy program a passing grade over all.

Mr. Wyden and other critics have questioned whether the assessments — in which the F.T.C. essentially outsources much of its day-to-day oversight to companies like PricewaterhouseCoopers — are effective. As with other businesses under consent agreements with the F.T.C., Facebook pays for and largely dictated the scope of its assessments, which are limited mostly to documenting that Facebook has conducted the internal privacy reviews it claims it had.

How closely Facebook monitored its data partners is uncertain. Most of Facebook's partners declined to discuss what kind of reviews or audits Facebook subjected them to. Two former Facebook partners, whose deals with the social network dated to 2010, said they could find no evidence that Facebook had ever audited them. One was Black-Berry. The other was Yandex.

Facebook officials said that while the social network audited partners only rarely, it managed them closely.

"These were high-touch relationships," Mr. Satterfield said.

MATTHEW ROSENBERG contributed reporting. Research was contributed by GRACE ASHFORD, SUSAN C. BEACHY, DORIS BURKE and ALAIN DELAQUÉRIÈRE.

Glossary

algorithm A precisely defined mathematical procedure for solving a problem, used extensively for navigating large data sets.

automation The process where tasks performed by humans are accomplished by machines, increasingly occurring in white-collar work.

circumspect Hesitant to take action or come to a definite conclusion on a matter.

clickbait A type of headline that teases or conceals an article's contents, often with the motivation of inflating site visits to generate advertising revenue.

collaborative filtering A method of generating recommendations based on similar users' preferences, frequently used in applications on the personalized web.

conspiracy theory A belief, often lacking credible evidence, in a conspiracy to cover up an event believed to have occurred.

echo chamber A pejorative term for communities with a limited range of viewpoints, often used in political conversations online.

e-commerce The use of the Internet to sell products and services.

fake news The phenomenon of biased, inflammatory or untrue news articles that circulate without editorial review or fact-checking.

Federal Trade Commission The primary regulatory body enforcing consumer protection laws.

filter bubble The phenomenon of the personalized web limiting one's media consumption to unchallenged preferences, originally coined by Eli Pariser in 2010.

Google bombing A more extreme form of search engine optimization, often associated with political campaigns and online pranks.

machine learning The use of algorithms to solve tasks without explicit instructions, often used in contemporary artificial intelligence.

megalomania An overstated sense of self-importance or power.

metrics The measurement of a site's or application's performance for the purpose of calculating advertising revenue.

monetize To convert something into a source of income, often applied to using web traffic to generate advertising revenue.

native advertising Advertising resembling ordinary content, such as videos or articles, with subtle references to a product or service.

news feed A feature on Facebook added in 2006, which collects posts in a personalized order for individual Facebook users.

pivot to video An ongoing shift in digital media, where publishers prioritize video production over written articles.

relevance A term used by tech companies to describe a user's personal interest in a piece of media, often made a priority of recommendation algorithms.

search engine optimization The practice of altering Google search results, where a search term is linked to a desired site by a number of other sites.

search term The words used in an Internet search, which search engines tag to a number of sites in order to rank them by relevance.

targeted advertising The tailoring of an advertisement to specific tastes or preferences, often filtered with user data.

user data The demographic, consumer and personal data collected by people who use a web platform, often sold to advertisers and other organizations.

web traffic The data gathered on the usage of a site, including number of visits and average time spent there per visitor.

Media Literacy Terms

"Media literacy" refers to the ability to access, understand, critically assess and create media. The following terms are important components of media literacy, and they will help you critically engage with the articles in this title.

angle The aspect of a news story that a journalist focuses on and develops.

attribution The method by which a source is identified or by which facts and information are assigned to the person who provided them.

balance Principle of journalism that both perspectives of an argument should be presented in a fair way.

bias A disposition of prejudice in favor of a certain idea, person or perspective.

byline Name of the writer, usually placed between the headline and the story.

chronological order Method of writing a story presenting the details of the story in the order in which they occurred.

credibility The quality of being trustworthy and believable, said of a journalistic source.

editorial Article of opinion or interpretation.

feature story Article designed to entertain as well as to inform.

headline Type, usually 18 point or larger, used to introduce a story.

human interest story Type of story that focuses on individuals and how events or issues affect their life, generally offering a sense of relatability to the reader.

impartiality Principle of journalism that a story should not reflect a journalist's bias and should contain balance.

intention The motive or reason behind something, such as the publication of a news story.

interview story Type of story in which the facts are gathered primarily by interviewing another person or persons.

inverted pyramid Method of writing a story using facts in order of importance, beginning with a lead and then gradually adding paragraphs in order of relevance from most interesting to least interesting.

motive The reason behind something, such as the publication of a news story or a source's perspective on an issue.

news story An article or style of expository writing that reports news, generally in a straightforward fashion and without editorial comment.

op-ed An opinion piece that reflects a prominent individual's opinion on a topic of interest.

paraphrase The summary of an individual's words, with attribution, rather than a direct quotation of their exact words.

quotation The use of an individual's exact words indicated by the use of quotation marks and proper attribution.

reliability The quality of being dependable and accurate, said of a journalistic source.

rhetorical device Technique in writing intending to persuade the reader or communicate a message from a certain perspective.

tone A manner of expression in writing or speech.

Media Literacy Questions

1. Look at the headline of "This Boring Headline Is Written for Google" (on page 10). How does the headline style reflect the article's observations? Compare it with other headlines in the book.

2. "If You Liked This, You're Sure to Love That" (on page 25) is a feature story about the rise of recommendations algorithms. What sources does Clive Thompson use to illustrate this technical topic? How do these sources make the story entertaining and relatable?

3. "F.T.C. Guidelines on Native Ads Aim to Prevent Deception" (on page 60) uses quotes from Henry Tajer, an advertising executive, and Jeffrey Chester, a critic calling for more advertising regulation. What perspective do each of these quotes provide for the story?

4. "Shocker! Facebook Changes Its Algorithm to Avoid 'Clickbait' " (on page 68) is written in inverted pyramid style, with the most important information placed first. Compare the first and last three paragraphs. What information did the authors believe was most important?

5. Eli Pariser's article, "When the Internet Thinks It Knows You" (on page 76), is an op-ed. What is Pariser's background, and how might it inform the article's core argument? What is the author's intention?

6. What is the tone of Burt Helm's article, "How Facebook's Oracular Algorithm Determines the Fates of Start-Ups" (on page 93)? How does Helm convey that tone? Consider the article's depiction of its interview subjects in your response.

7. What is the angle of Natalie Kitroeff's article, "Why That Video Went Viral" (on page 110)? How do the other news sources cited in the article contribute to that angle?

8. Sapna Maheshwari's article, "On YouTube Kids, Startling Videos Slip Past Filters" (on page 117), is a human interest story. What audience is the article likely meant to appeal to?

9. Compare Farhad Manjoo's article, "Facebook's Bias Is Built-In, and Bears Watching" (on page 142), with Ross Douthat's article, "Facebook's Subtle Empire" (on page 148). Manjoo, a progressive author, and Douthat, a conservative author, are both writing about allegations of political bias at Facebook. How does each author address the allegation, and how does each strive for balance in his article?

10. "Facebook and the Digital Virus Called Fake News" (on page 164) is an editorial. How is the byline of the editorial different from other bylines, and what is the intention of the article?

11. "Can Facebook Fix Its Own Worst Bug?" (on page 177) is a feature story about Facebook C.E.O. Mark Zuckerberg, written in chronological order. How does the order contribute to its depiction of Zuckerberg's attempts to address Facebook's critics?

12. "As Facebook Raised a Privacy Wall, It Carved an Opening for Tech Giants" (on page 199) uses document sources in its investigative report on Facebook and data privacy. How does the article interpret and contextualize these sources?

Citations

All citations in this list are formatted according to the Modern Language Association's (MLA) style guide.

BOOK CITATION

THE NEW YORK TIMES EDITORIAL STAFF. *Filter Bubbles and Targeted Advertising*. New York: New York Times Educational Publishing, 2020.

ONLINE ARTICLE CITATIONS

CARR, DAVID. "Risks Abound as Reporters Play in Traffic." *The New York Times*, 23 Mar. 2014, https://www.nytimes.com/2014/03/24/business /media/risks-abound-as-reporters-play-in-traffic.html.

DANCE, GABRIEL J.X., ET AL. "As Facebook Raised a Privacy Wall, It Carved an Opening for Tech Giants." *The New York Times*, 18 Dec. 2018, https://www .nytimes.com/2018/12/18/technology/facebook-privacy.html.

DOUTHAT, ROSS. "Facebook's Subtle Empire." *The New York Times*, 21 May 2016, https://www.nytimes.com/2016/05/22/opinion/sunday/facebooks -subtle-empire.html.

EMBER, SYDNEY. "F.T.C. Guidelines on Native Ads Aim to Prevent Deception." *The New York Times*, 22 Dec. 2015, https://www.nytimes.com/2015/12/23 /business/media/ftc-issues-guidelines-for-native-ads.html.

FISHER, MAX, AND KATRIN BENNHOLD. "As Germans Seek News, YouTube Delivers Far-Right Tirades." *The New York Times*, 7 Sept. 2018, https:// www.nytimes.com/2018/09/07/world/europe/youtube-far-right-extremism .html.

HELM, BURT. "How Facebook's Oracular Algorithm Determines the Fate of Start-Ups." *The New York Times*, 2 Nov. 2017, https://www.nytimes.com /2017/11/02/magazine/how-facebooks-oracular-algorithm-determines-the -fates-of-start-ups.html.

HERRMAN, JOHN. "Facebook's Problem Isn't Fake News — It's the Rest of the

Internet." *The New York Times*, 22 Dec. 2016, https://www.nytimes .com/2016/12/22/magazine/facebooks-problem-isnt-fake-news-its-the-rest -of-the-internet.html.

HERRMAN, JOHN. "How Sponsored Content Is Becoming King in a Facebook World." *The New York Times*, 24 June 2016, https://www.nytimes.com /2016/07/25/business/sponsored-content-takes-larger-role-in-media -companies.html.

HERRMAN, JOHN. "Inside Facebook's (Totally Insane, Unintentionally Gigantic, Hyperpartisan) Political-Media Machine." *The New York Times*, 24 Aug. 2016, https://www.nytimes.com/2016/08/28/magazine/inside-facebooks -totally-insane-unintentionally-gigantic-hyperpartisan-political-media -machine.html.

ISAAC, MIKE, AND SYDNEY EMBER. "Shocker! Facebook Changes Its Algorithm to Avoid 'Clickbait.'" *The New York Times*, 4 Aug. 2016, https://www .nytimes.com/2016/08/05/technology/facebook-moves-to-push-clickbait -lower-in-the-news-feed.html.

KANG, CECILIA. "YouTube Kids App Faces New Complaints Over Ads for Junk Food." *The New York Times*, 24 Nov. 2015, https://www.nytimes .com/2015/11/25/technology/youtube-kids-app-faces-new-complaints.html.

KITROEFF, NATALIE. "Why That Video Went Viral." *The New York Times*, 19 May 2014, https://www.nytimes.com/2014/05/20/science/why-that -video-went-viral.html.

LOHR, STEVE. "This Boring Headline Is Written for Google." *The New York Times*, 9 Apr. 2006, https://www.nytimes.com/2006/04/09 /weekinreview/ideas-trends-this-boring-headline-is-written-for -google.html.

MAHESHWARI, SAPNA. "New Pressure on Google and YouTube Over Children's Data." *The New York Times*, 20 Sept. 2018, https://www.nytimes.com /2018/09/20/business/media/google-youtube-children-data.html.

MAHESHWARI, SAPNA. "On YouTube Kids, Startling Videos Slip Past Filters." *The New York Times*, 4 Nov. 2017, https://www.nytimes.com/2017/11/04 /business/media/youtube-kids-paw-patrol.html.

MAHESHWARI, SAPNA, AND ALEXANDRA STEVENSON. "Google and Facebook Face Criticism for Ads Targeting Racist Sentiments." *The New York Times*, 15 Sept. 2017, https://www.nytimes.com/2017/09/15/business/facebook -advertising-anti-semitism.html.

MANJOO, FARHAD. "Can Facebook Fix Its Own Worst Bug?" *The New York*

Times, 25 Apr. 2017, https://www.nytimes.com/2017/04/25/magazine/can
-facebook-fix-its-own-worst-bug.html.

MANJOO, FARHAD. "Facebook's Bias Is Built-In, and Bears Watching." *The New
York Times*, 11 May 2016, https://www.nytimes.com/2016/05/12/technology
/facebooks-bias-is-built-in-and-bears-watching.html.

MARKOFF, JOHN. "Researchers Track Down a Plague of Fake Web Pages."
The New York Times, 19 Mar. 2007, https://www.nytimes.com/2007/03/19
/technology/19spam.html.

THE NEW YORK TIMES. "Facebook and the Digital Virus Called Fake News."
The New York Times, 19 Nov. 2016, https://www.nytimes.com/2016/11
/20/opinion/sunday/facebook-and-the-digital-virus-called-fake-news
.html.

THE NEW YORK TIMES. "The Google Algorithm." *The New York Times*,
14 July 2010, https://www.nytimes.com/2010/07/15/opinion/15thu3.html.

PARISER, ELI. "When the Internet Thinks It Knows You." *The New York
Times*, 22 May 2011, https://www.nytimes.com/2011/05/23/opinion
/23pariser.html.

ROOSE, KEVIN. "YouTube Unleashed a Conspiracy Theory Boom. Can It Be
Contained?" *The New York Times*, 19 Feb. 2019, https://www.nytimes
.com/2019/02/19/technology/youtube-conspiracy-stars.html.

SAFRONOVA, VALERIYA. "What the 'Pivot to Video' Looks Like at Condé Nast."
The New York Times, 4 Apr. 2018, https://www.nytimes.com/2018/04/04
/style/conde-nast-bon-appetit-food-video.html.

SEGAL, DAVID. "Arianna Huffington's Improbable, Insatiable Content
Machine." *The New York Times*, 30 June 2015, https://www.nytimes.com
/2015/07/05/magazine/arianna-huffingtons-improbable-insatiable
-content-machine.html.

SENGUPTA, SOMINI. "What You Didn't Post, Facebook May Still Know."
The New York Times, 25 Mar. 2013, https://www.nytimes.com/2013/03/26
/technology/facebook-expands-targeted-advertising-through-outside
-data-sources.html.

SINGER, NATASHA. "Just Don't Call It Privacy." *The New York Times*, 22 Sept.
2018, https://www.nytimes.com/2018/09/22/sunday-review/privacy
-hearing-amazon-google.html.

SINGER, NATASHA. "The Trouble With the Echo Chamber Online." *The New
York Times*, 28 May 2011, https://www.nytimes.com/2011/05/29
/technology/29stream.html.

TABUCHI, HIROKO. "How Climate Change Deniers Rise to the Top in Google Searches." *The New York Times*, 29 Dec. 2017, https://www.nytimes.com /2017/12/29/climate/google-search-climate-change.html.

TAUB, ERIC A. "Guessing the Online Customer's Next Want." *The New York Times*, 19 May 2008, https://www.nytimes.com/2008/05/19/technology /19recommend.html.

THOMPSON, CLIVE. "If You Liked This, You're Sure to Love That." *The New York Times*, 21 Nov. 2008, https://www.nytimes.com/2008/11/23 /magazine/23Netflix-t.html.

WU, TIM. "Good at Skipping Ads? No, You're Not." *The New York Times*, 25 Nov. 2016, https://www.nytimes.com/2016/11/25/books/review /black-ops-advertising-mara-einstein.html.

ZELLER, TOM, JR. "A New Campaign Tactic: Manipulating Google Data." *The New York Times*, 26 Oct. 2006, https://www.nytimes.com/2006/10/26/us /politics/26googlebomb.html.

Index

This book is current up until the time of printing. For the most up-to-date reporting, visit www.nytimes.com.